TRANSLATIONS FROM GREEK AND ROMAN AUTHORS
Series Editor: GRAHAM TINGAY

VIRGIL

Selections from the *Aeneid*

Translated by

GRAHAM TINGAY

Head of Classics, King's College School, Wimbledon

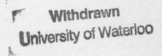

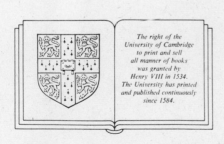

The right of the
University of Cambridge
to print and sell
all manner of books
was granted by
Henry VIII in 1534.
The University has printed
and published continuously
since 1584.

CAMBRIDGE UNIVERSITY PRESS

Cambridge
London   New York   New Rochelle
Melbourne   Sydney

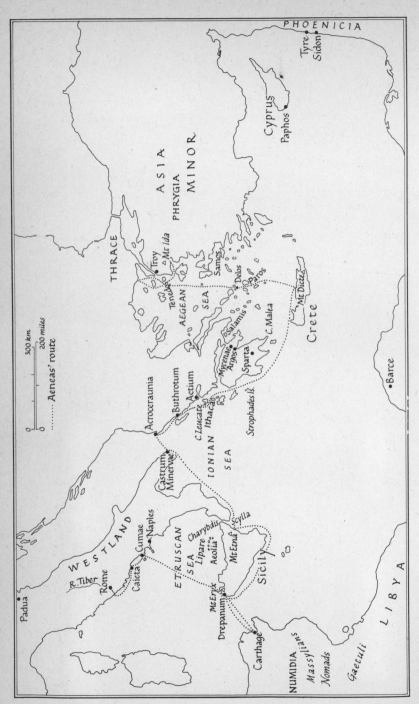

The voyage of Aeneas

Contents

Introduction   *page* 4

Book I   9

Book II   32

Book III   55

Book IV   60

Book V   83

Book VI   93

Book VII   111

Book VIII   120

Book IX   130

Book X   136

Book XI   146

Book XII   153

Maps

1. The voyage of Aeneas   2

2. Central Italy   110

Passages translated

Book I	1–440		268–81	Book X	100–17
	494–735		295–332		260–314
	748–56		384–476		440–504
Book II	1–361		555–600		769–908
	370–434		608–64	Book XI	100–21
	469–95		679–723		281–93
	506–623		752–66		434–42
	671–804		847–53		498–519
Book III	588–683	Book VII	293–304		648–58
	707–18		308–94		664–8
Book IV	1–705		406–537		690–720
Book V	104–243		540–8		732–40
	268–81		805–17		758–67
	315–61	Book VIII	310–36		778–806
	604–63		359–69		816–31
	676–99		423–53	Book XII	1–17
Book VI	1–13		470–517		54–80
	42–148		617–731		696–790
	190–211	Book IX	168–223		818–42
	236–63		354–445		887–952

Introduction

The *Aeneid*

When Virgil lay desperately ill and on the point of death he kept on asking for the manuscript of the *Aeneid*, in order to burn it – he had barely started the three years' revision which he thought the poem needed. But no one brought it to him, and soon after Virgil's death the emperor Augustus had the poem published. He knew Virgil well and admired his work; the three books of the *Aeneid* which Virgil had read to him had convinced him that the whole poem must be preserved. Over the last two thousand years no one has ever had any serious doubts that Augustus was right. It is for the *Aeneid*, above all else, that Virgil is still regarded as the greatest of Roman poets, indeed one of the greatest poets of all time.

The *Aeneid* is an 'epic poem', a name given to a long straightforward and rapid account of heroic adventures, in which both men and gods are closely involved. (The two most famous examples of epic poems are the *Iliad* and the *Odyssey* by Homer.) Of the men, the most important characters are 'heroes', larger-than-life princes or kings, whose thoughts and actions are governed by strict unwritten laws of chivalry: the very reason for their lives is to fight bravely in battle, if necessary to die bravely. But Aeneas is different from other heroes: he is not allowed to earn his heroic reputation by dying in battle. The *Aeneid* tells how, after the destruction of Troy by the Greeks, Aeneas, a prince of the city, struggles through countless difficulties to reach Italy, and wins in war the right to build a new home for his people; from this settlement grew the Roman people and the Roman empire.

Virgil

Virgil was born at Andes, a village near Mantua in northern Italy in 70 BC; both the time and the place had a marked influence on everything he wrote. He was a farmer's son, and his personal knowledge of country life, and his love of the romantic north Italian countryside, are constantly reflected in his poetry. He was educated at Cremona, then Milan and Rome, where he met some of the men who were to take an important part in the political life of his country.

His youth was overshadowed first by political unrest in Italy, then by a grim civil war fought between Julius Caesar and Pompey. Italy was devastated by bitter fighting when another civil war broke out soon after Caesar's murder in 44 BC. By 42 BC Mark Antony (Caesar's second-in-command) and Octavian (Caesar's young heir) had won a major victory over those who had opposed Caesar. Antony went to reorganise the eastern half of the empire, and became involved with Cleopatra.

Virgil felt the full force of the war, for his father's farm was confiscated soon after 42 BC to provide land for the demobilised veteran soldiers, and he spent the rest of his life in Rome or Naples. Though his poetry soon won him a measure of fame and financial security, he never forgot the horror and waste of war.

Virgil's poetry

The first poems were the *Eclogues*, ten short pastoral poems begun in 42 and published in 37 BC. The calm peaceful scenes of rustic life which they describe were a conventional topic that had little to do with the real life of Italian shepherds of the time. Virgil had become a member of a famous literary circle – Horace and Propertius were to join it later – under the patronage of Maecenas, a friend and colleague of Octavian. At Maecenas' suggestion, between 37 and 30 BC, Virgil wrote the *Georgics*, four short books which give a poetic account of Italian farming. Their success and charm derive from Virgil's own delight in rural life, and from his sympathy with the object of the poems, to revive the simple tastes and virtues of an earlier, less complicated, age.

Before the publication of the *Georgics*, fighting on a huge scale had broken out again when Octavian and Antony turned against each other. By 30 BC Antony and Cleopatra were dead, and Octavian had emerged as the undisputed master of the Roman world, and with his victory had at last brought an end to war. It is easy to see why Octavian (who was soon to be given the name Augustus by which he has been known ever since) was looked up to with so much hope by Virgil and his contemporaries: he offered them the peace and stability which had been missing for so long: he promised a return to the morality and religion which the wars had banished, a return to a new Golden Age. Small wonder in this climate of gathering hope that poets like Virgil, and historians like Livy, looked for ways to help in recalling the patriotic virtues of the past. Virgil spent the rest of his life, from some time after 30 BC till his death in 19 BC, writing the *Aeneid*.

Aeneas, duty and Fate

By returning to the legend of Aeneas' arrival in Italy for the subject of his poem, Virgil could link the history of his Rome to the most glorious 'historical' period of the past, that of the Trojan War as narrated in Homer's *Iliad* and *Odyssey*. These two poems were the first literature to appear in western civilisation: their success was overwhelming, their characters and their gods dominated the literature and religion of Greece and Rome ever afterwards. By connecting Rome to the early

5

Greeks and their heroes, Virgil could in some way give Rome a share in their greatness. In various forms of prophecy (e.g. the visit to the Underworld in Book VI, the scenes on Aeneas' shield in Book VIII), by pointing out similarities or derivations (e.g. the names of the captains in the Boat Race in Book V), Rome's present and past could be explained and related. The noble character of Aeneas could typify the best Roman character; Aeneas could be compared to Augustus; Augustus' family, the Julian *gens* whose patron goddess was Venus, could gain especial glory.

Again and again Virgil uses the Latin words *pius* and *pietas* ('dutiful', 'duty') when describing Aeneas. They are difficult to put into comfortable English, but emphasise Aeneas' attitude to his mission. Duty, to one's country, to one's gods, to what is right, was also the virtue that Augustus, and Virgil, regarded as of the highest importance for the recovery of Rome's greatness and for her future growth. Aeneas, too, is constantly shown to be aware of Fate, a force steering him towards his goal: it is a reflection of Virgil's own belief in the fate of Rome, in the destiny of its people as rulers of the world, a belief that, directly or indirectly, is implicit throughout the poem.

❦❦❦❦

One of the most striking features of the *Aeneid* is the view that Italy will be a single nation, embracing all its different peoples and tribes in justice and equality. In fact Italy had only just become united when the *Aeneid* was being written. When Virgil was born his home town was part of a province known as Cisalpine Gaul: it was not incorporated in Roman Italy until 42 BC. Equally impressive is the belief that Rome's history is a continuous stream from the first landing by the mouth of the Tiber to the full expansion of the empire. These were themes that immediately captured the imagination of the Roman people. Moreover, they were expressed in grand yet exciting language, enhanced by Virgil's sympathy for human suffering, his penetrating observation of nature and his faith in the infinite nobility of mankind. But above all it is as a first-rate story that the *Aeneid* has been most easily enjoyed, and perhaps always will be.

The translation

It is inevitable that this selection will satisfy no one completely, that everyone will find a favourite passage missing – as are many of mine. But I wanted to offer an intelligible version of the narrative of the whole *Aeneid*, rather than one of the divisions that have appeared before, e.g. Books I–IV, I–VI or V–VIII, so much had to be omitted. Most of Books I, II and IV appears, with half of VI and enough, I hope, of each of the others to show its particular quality or place in the structure of the whole. In all there are some 4,200 lines out of the total 9,896.

I found that the English constantly fell *sua sponte* into a rhythm not unlike parts of a hexameter; though this was not intentional, I have consciously been looking for a version that would sound well when read aloud. I hope that you will be tempted to try.

A summary introduces each Book, often ending with a comment about the nature of the Book. Short summaries in the text explain passages omitted or what follows, though the omission of a few phrases or sentences has not been indicated. Small raised numbers in the text – e.g. 'more even than Samos[2]' – refer to explanatory notes at the end of each Book.

My most grateful thanks are due to Dr J.G. Henderson of King's College, Cambridge, for many inspired suggestions, and for saving me from a host of errors: my own folly and obstinacy are responsible for those that remain.

The Trojan War

Once upon a time the marriage feast of Peleus and Thetis was attended by all the gods and goddesses but one, Eris, goddess of Discord. She came to the door and threw in a golden apple, inscribed 'for the fairest'. It was claimed by three goddesses, Juno, the wife of Jupiter, and Athena and Venus, his daughters (by different wives). When Jupiter wisely declined to adjudicate, they went to the handsomest of mortals, Paris, son of Priam, king of Troy, and asked him to decide. Juno offered him greatness, Athena success in war, and Venus the loveliest woman for his wife. The apple was, of course, awarded to Venus, even though this 'Judgement of Paris' found little favour with the other two.

The most beautiful woman in the world was Helen, daughter of Zeus and Leda. All the kings and chiefs of Greece wanted to marry her, but agreed to accept her choice, and to defend her husband. She picked Menelaus, king of Sparta. Paris sailed for Sparta, and with the aid of Venus won Helen's heart when Menelaus was away, and sailed back with her to Troy.

All the kings and princes of Greece, under the leadership of Agamemnon, king of Mycenae, Menelaus' brother, assembled at Aulis in a huge army, to recover Helen. However, for six weeks an adverse wind prevented them sailing till Agamemnon, on the advice of the prophet Calchas, sacrificed his daughter Iphigenia. At once the wind changed and the fleet sailed.

For nine years the fighting was indecisive; then followed the events described in the *Iliad* by Homer. A plague had broken out in the Greek camp: Calchas declared that it would not stop unless Agamemnon gave back his prize, the maiden Chryseis, to her father, priest of Apollo. Agamemnon reluctantly did so, but took in her place a slave-girl belonging to Achilles. Achilles was the greatest of the Greek warriors, and he refused to take any further part in the war. Deprived of his support, the Greeks were almost defeated. Even when Agamemnon offered to make amends Achilles refused, and said he would sail home on the next day. His friend Patroclus, ashamed by Achilles' stubbornness, donned Achilles' armour and went out to fight, but was killed by Priam's son Hector, the leading Trojan warrior.

At last Achilles, in remorse for his own selfish anger, put on new armour, and rejoining the battle he killed Hector. Forgetting the chivalrous conduct expected of heroes, he treated the dead body with cruel outrage; when Priam came to ask for his son's body Achilles relented and returned it to him.

Soon afterwards Troy fell to the Greeks, as Virgil relates. One of the Trojan survivors was Prince Aeneas.

Book I

Aeneas is the leader of a tired band of Trojan refugees. For seven years since the fall of Troy they have been wandering round the Mediterranean in search of a new home, which they have recently learnt will be in Italy. They have just left Sicily, believing that they are on the last stage of their journey. But the goddess Juno understands that it is fated that a race descended from the Trojans will one day destroy her beloved city of Carthage, so she asks Aeolus, the god of the winds, to let loose a storm on Aeneas' fleet. Some ships are wrecked, the rest are scattered. Aeneas manages to reach the coast of Libya, where he is met by his mother Venus, disguised as a huntress. She tells him to make for the city of Carthage. He is there welcomed by Queen Dido, and reunited with the rest of his followers who have survived the storm. Dido invites the Trojans to a great banquet, where Venus, in collusion with Juno, arranges that Dido shall fall in love with Aeneas. She asks him to tell her how Troy was captured, and of all he has been through since then.

Characters

Gods
Jupiter, also known as Jove, king of the gods
Juno, his wife; she is bitterly opposed to the Trojans, and friendly to the Carthaginians
Venus, daughter of Jupiter, mother of Aeneas
Cupid, her son
Neptune, god of water and the sea
Aeolus, god of the winds

Trojans
Aeneas, a Trojan prince, son of Anchises and the goddess Venus
Ascanius, also known as Iulus, son of Aeneas
Achates, lieutenant of Aeneas

Tyrian
Dido, Queen of Carthage, who had fled from Tyre

Places

Troy, a city in Phrygia (north-west Turkey)
Olympus, home of the gods
Tyre, a city in Phoenicia (Lebanon)
Lavinium, a town built by Aeneas in Latium, a district in central
    Italy
Carthage, a city built by Dido on the north coast of Africa, which
    Virgil sometimes calls Libya (though it is in modern
    Tunisia)

 1–11   Virgil announces that the subject of his poem is the
struggle of a hero from Troy to found a new race in Italy, and
calls upon the Muse-goddess of poetry to tell why the queen of the
gods is so opposed to his efforts.

I tell a story of war and a hero. He was a refugee chased by Fate[1]
from the land of Troy, first to reach Italy where Lavinium was to
be built. Time and again he was driven over land and sea by the
might of the gods – all because Juno was cruel and angry, slow to
forget. He endured many hardships in war as well, until he could
build a city and install his gods in Latium. Out of all this came
the Latin people, our forefathers in Alba and the walls of great
Rome.

Explain for me, Muse, the reasons; for what blow to her pride,
what hurt to her feelings, did Juno, queen of the gods, make the
hero, whose devotion to duty so marked him out, undergo such a
string of disasters, such countless ordeals? Can there be so much
anger in the hearts of the gods?

12–33   Juno hates the Trojans because they are destined to
destroy Carthage, her favourite city, and because Paris, prince of
Troy, when asked to award the prize for beauty between Juno,
Athena and Venus, chose Venus.

The ancient city of Carthage, which settlers from Tyre colonised,
lay opposite Italy and the distant mouth of the Tiber. It was rich
and powerful, pugnacious and practised in war, and Juno is said
to have loved it above all others, more even than Samos.[2] Here

10

stood her statue, riding armed in her chariot. Long ago she had set her heart on making Carthage supreme in the world, if only Fate would allow it. Yet she had heard that a new race, rising from Trojan blood, would one day overthrow Carthage, that this people would rule far and wide, and, proud in war, come to destroy all her African kingdom, for so the Fates had decided.

In fear of this, and remembering the old war at Troy which she had fought from the first for the Greeks she loved (moreover the causes of her anger and bitter resentment were still fresh in Juno's mind: deep in her heart she brooded on the Judgement of Paris, his contempt for her beauty, the Trojans she hated, and Jupiter's theft of the boy Ganymede[3] to serve him), inflamed by all this she tossed the Trojans about all over the seas, and kept them, those that escaped the Greeks and Achilles' pitiless vengeance, far from Latium. For years on end they wandered the oceans, harried by destiny. So immense was the task of founding the Roman race!

34–80   Juno broods on her humiliation, then visits the god of the winds and gets him to wreck Aeneas' fleet for her.

The Trojans had only just lost sight of Sicily, happily sailing towards deep water, churning the sea into foam with their bronze-clad prows, when Juno, still nursing deep in her heart her endless resentment, said to herself. 'Have *I* been beaten? Must *I* give up, and fail to keep the Trojan king out of Italy? "It's forbidden by Fate", I suppose! Athena could burn the ships of the Greeks and drown their crews for nothing more than one man's criminal madness when Ajax assaulted Cassandra.[4] Down from the clouds *she* hurled Jove's bolt of lightning, ravaged the seas with gales and shattered their boats. Ajax himself, gasping flames from his gaping chest, she snatched up in a whirlwind and impaled on a needle of rock. But I, who walk majestic as queen of the gods, both sister and wife to Jove, must battle for years on end with just one race! Does anyone respect my power any more? Will anyone bring offerings to my altar to ask for my help?'

With such thoughts spinning around in her heart, burning with anger, the goddess came to Aeolia, home of the clouds, the island which spawns impetuous winds. Here in a massive cave Aeolus holds down the battling winds and thunderous storms with royal authority, curbs them with chains and bars. The gales fume and fret at the bolts that restrain them, while the mountain rumbles and roars. Aeolus sits enthroned in his citadel, grasping his sceptre, soothing their passions and calming their tantrums. Without his control the winds would whirl along with them lands, seas and infinite heaven, and sweep them away into space. Fearing that this might happen, the all-powerful Father buried them deep in darkness and dungeon, towered the mass of a mountain above them, and gave them a ruler with rigid instructions to tighten or loosen their reins, as ordered. So it was that Juno came to beg Aeolus' help in these words.

'Aeolus, the Father and king of gods and men appointed you to quieten the waves or arouse them with gales. A race I loathe is sailing the Etruscan sea, bringing Troy and its defeated gods to Italy. So give your winds violence – sink all their ships without trace, drive the Trojans in every direction, scatter their corpses all over the sea! I have fourteen gorgeous Nymphs⁵ to serve me: in return for your kindness I'll give you in lasting marriage the one with the greatest beauty, and pronounce her yours, to spend the rest of her years by your side, and make you the father of beautiful children.'

The god of the winds replied: 'Your majesty, you must decide what you wish: my role is to carry out orders. This humble kingdom of mine, this sceptre, Jupiter's good will towards me, were all won for me by you; it is you who allow me to join the gods at their feasts, and make me master of tempest and cloud.'

81–101   Aeneas, caught in the frightening storm which Aeolus has aroused, regrets that he did not die at Troy.

As Aeolus spoke he drove his spear-butt at the hollow mountain's side; the winds line up like an army ready to march, and speed through the exit he's made. Hurricanes scour the earth's surface. Then together the East Wind, South and Sou'wester, bursting with squall after squall, crash down on the sea, scoop it up from its depths, and roll it in mighty waves to the shore. Next come the shouts of the men and the shriek of the wind in the rigging. Storm-clouds suddenly steal sky and daylight from the eyes of the Trojans: black night looms over the sea, the heavens crack with thunder and flickering lightning flashes. Everything threatens the men with immediate death.

In an instant Aeneas' limbs grow cold and weak. With a groan he lifts both hands to the stars, and calls out: 'You were the lucky ones, three times lucky and more, who had the good fortune to die under the walls of Troy, before the eyes of your fathers! Why couldn't I have died and yielded my soul to the sword of Diomede,[6] bravest of Greeks, on the Trojan plains, where grim Hector fell to the spear of Achilles, where mighty Sarpedon[7] died, where the river Simois clutches the helmets and shields and bodies of heroes, and rolls them along in its depths?'

102–23   Aeneas' fleet is scattered and wrecked by the fury of the storm.

So Aeneas cries out, and a squall, shrieking down from the north, smacks straight into his sail, and stacks up the seas sky-high. Oars snap with a bang, then the bows lurch round, presenting the side of the ship to the waves, and a great steep mountain of water piles up behind. One ship hangs poised on the crest of a wave; to another the seas, yawning open, disclose the bottom in the trough of the waves, and the sand boils up in the brine. Three ships the South Wind seizes and hurls onto submerged rocks – the Italians call them the Altars, a dangerous reef in the middle of the sea, lurking just under the surface. Three more ships the East Wind drives from the deep into the shallows and shoals – a pitiful sight – and batters them onto the land's edge and builds up a dam of sand around them.

Even as Aeneas watches, a huge wave crashes down sheer on the stern of the vessel carrying the Lycians and trusty Orontes,[8] and the helmsman is tossed overboard head first; as for the vessel itself, three times in the selfsame spot the billow violently spins it around before the raging whirlpool sucks it down to the depths. Here and there a swimmer appears, dwarfed by the turmoil, with weapons of war, planks, Trojan treasure littering the waves. Now Ilioneus' stout craft, and the ships of valiant Achates, and of Abas and aged Aletes, succumb to the storm: the timbers spring loose, split open and crack, and let in the deadly water.

124–41   Neptune god of the sea intervenes to help the Trojans.

Meanwhile Neptune has sensed that his ocean is churned to chaotic confusion, that a storm is let loose, that still waters have surged up from the sea-bed. Sorely troubled, he lifts his head from the wave-tops, looking out over the ocean in majestic serenity. His eye falls on Aeneas' fleet, scattered all over the surface, and the Trojans overwhelmed by the waves and the ruins of heaven. The spiteful tricks of Juno, his sister, do not escape him. He summons the East Wind, and the West Wind, and then says: 'Are you so emboldened by family pride that you dare, you winds, without permission from me, your god, to plunge both earth and sky into turmoil, to raise such masses of water? Why, I'll – but better, first, to calm the storm; later you'll not get away so lightly with crimes such as these. Off with you, quick! – and tell your king this: command of the seas, this fearful trident, was allotted to me, not him. He rules that mountain of rock where you live, East Wind; let King Aeolus lord it there in his castle, and keep the winds locked up in their prison.'

142–56   The god of the sea rescues the stranded ships.

He spoke, and quicker than speech he quietens the restless water, rounds up the clouds and dismisses them, and brings back the sun. The sea-nymph Cymothoe and Neptune's son Triton, heaving together, dislodge the ships from the sharp sea-rocks; Neptune himself with his trident lifts off the others, opens a path through the endless sandbanks, levels the waters, and skims lightly across the wave-tops in his chariot.

Often, when there's a large crowd, rioting breaks out; tempers flare in the ugly mob and burning sticks and stones go flying as their madness finds itself missiles – then if they catch sight of a man of distinction and authority, whom they respect, they fall silent and stand there eager to listen, and his words rule their minds and calm down their passions. It was like this when the whole sea fell quiet, once the Father of Ocean, riding through the clearing sky, gazed out over the waves, wheeled round his horses, gave them their head and drove swiftly away.

157–79   Aeneas' men, huddling exhausted on the shore, start a
fire and prepare a meal.

Worn out, the Trojans hurriedly make for the nearest land, and
turn towards Libya's coast. There's a place there in a deep bay; a
natural harbour is formed by an island barring the entrance, and
the waves, rolling in from the ocean, break on the island's shore,
divide and swirl up each inlet. There's a cliff of huge boulders
where a pair of great rocks rear threateningly into the sky, but
below them the water is still and safe. Above, the stage is set with
a curtain of quivering trees – a dark wood, overhanging, with
unsettling shadows. Straight ahead under the cliff face is a cave
hung with stalactites; inside fresh water and natural rock,
forming seats – it's the home of the sea-nymphs. Here tired ships
need no cable, nor hooked bite of anchor to hold them. Here
Aeneas put in with all seven ships that were left of his fleet. With
a passionate craving for dry land the Trojans spilled out, took
possession of the sands they'd longed for, and stretched out their
limbs, encrusted with salt, on the shore.
    First, Achates struck a spark from flint, helped on the fire with
leaves, fed it dry twigs all around, and whipped up the flames
with kindling. Next, worn out though they were, they got out the
wave-damaged corn and the utensils for baking, intending to dry
by the fire this grain they had salvaged and grind it to flour.

180–222   Aeneas looks out for other survivors, but instead finds
meat for his men, whom he tries to encourage.

Meanwhile Aeneas climbed up a rock, looking for a good view
out over the sea, in the hope of seeing Trojan ships, a storm-
tossed Antheus[9] perhaps, or Capys, or Caicus' shield fixed high
on the stern. No ship in sight, but his eye was caught by three
stags rambling along the shore, and behind them the whole herd
in a long line, browsing through the dunes. Aeneas steadied
himself, caught up the bow and arrows which trusty Achates
carried, shot down the leaders first as they held their heads high
with their branching antlers, then harried the rest of the herd
with his shafts and scattered them into the leafy woodland. He
kept on shooting till he'd triumphantly stretched on the ground

15

seven great carcasses – one for each of the ships. Then he made his way back to the harbour and distributed them among his comrades. Next he shared out the casks of wine which the noble Acestes[10] had filled on the shores of Sicily and given them as they were leaving. Last, Aeneas said something to soothe their sorrowing hearts.

'My friends, we've known troubles enough in the past, and we've suffered still worse: god *will* bring an end to these too. You sailed right past that mad fiend Scylla[11] and her deeply resounding cavern: you survived the Cyclops'[12] rocks. Cheer up! Enough of sorrow and fear! One day, perhaps, even this will be something good to remember. Whatever the disasters we meet, whatever the crises we go through, our goal is Latium! The Fates point to a home for us there, and peace. There a kingdom of Troy can rise once again. Don't give up now! Save yourselves for the good things to come!'

These were Aeneas' words. Though sick with crushing anxiety, he put on a confident look and buried the grief deep in his heart. Some of the men set to work on the game for their banquet, ripping the hides off the ribs of the deer, disclosing the flesh. Then some cut the meat into chunks, and thrust it still quivering onto spits, while others set up pots on the beach, building up fires beneath them. The food gave them back their strength, and they sprawled on the grass filling themselves with old wine and rich venison. When their hunger was satisfied and the feast cleared away, wavering between hope and fear, they passed the hours in talk, lamenting the loss of their friends – should they believe them alive, still dying, or dead? Noble Aeneas grieved more than them all for his followers, for the doom of stout-hearted Orontes[13] and Amycus, for the cruel fate of Lycus, for brave Gyas and brave Cloanthus.

223–41   As the action among men pauses, Virgil turns his attention to the gods. Venus begs Jupiter to let Aeneas reach Italy at last.

So much for the Trojans. Jupiter was looking down from the height of heaven on the sail-studded sea and the lands far below, with their shores and wide-spread peoples: at the pinnacle of heaven he paused, his eyes fixed down on the realms of Libya. As he mused feelingly over the troubles below, Venus, grim-faced for once, eyes bright with welling tears, spoke to him: 'Lord, men and gods alike are ruled for ever by your commands, and awed by your lightning. What can my Aeneas, what can his Trojans have done so terribly wrong, that, despite all the deaths they have suffered, you bar the whole world against them, to stop them reaching Italy? From them, so you promised, there would one day come, as the years rolled by, the leaders of Rome, reviving the blood of Troy, to hold the whole world and the sea in their sway. Father, why have you changed your mind? I comforted myself over the sack of Troy, over its grim devastation, by weighing its future good fortune against its past ill luck: yet still my heroes are dogged by the same fate, despite all the disasters they've suffered. When *will* you grant them an end to their trials?'

242–53   Venus asks why another Trojan hero has been able to come safely to his new home in north Italy while Aeneas, her own son, is still unsuccessful.

'Antenor managed to slip through the clutches of the Greeks, to sail north between Greece and Italy despite all the trials of the journey, and found a new city, Padua, a home for *his* Trojans. He has given his name to a race, and laid up *his* Trojan arms, calmly settled in peace and quiet. But Aeneas and I, your offspring, to whom you promise a place in the citadel of heaven, because of one person's anger we have lost our ships – it's monstrous! – we're betrayed and banished far from our home in Italy! Is this the reward for our dutiful devotion? Is this how you restore us to royal power?'

254–96   To comfort Venus, Jupiter tells her what is fated to happen: Aeneas *will* found his city; Roman descendants of the Trojans *will* rule the world; Julius, a descendant of Aeneas, *will* rule the Roman empire; peace on earth *will* one day prevail.

The Father of gods and men, smiling at his daughter with the expression that calms the stormiest sky, kissed her lightly on the lips and said, 'Don't be afraid; the fate of your people remains unchanged. You *shall* see the city you were promised, and the walls of Lavinium; you *shall* bring your great-hearted Aeneas up to the stars to join us gods. I have *not* changed my mind. You'll see – for I'm now going to tell you more fully, since you are tortured by doubt; I will reveal the mysteries held in the book of Fate.

'Aeneas will fight a great war in Italy, crushing fierce tribes, and establish for his people a city, and a civilised code of conduct. Three summers and winters will he rule in Latium once he has conquered the Rutuli. His young son Ascanius, now also called Iulus (he was Ilus while Ilium's rule was intact), will reign full thirty years with all their months rolling by, moving the throne from Lavinium to build the mighty town of Long Alba. Here for three hundred years will reign the children of Troy, till Ilia, a priestess-queen pregnant by Mars, shall bear twin sons. Then Romulus, proud in the tawny skin of the wolf that nursed him, will take over the race, found the city of Mars, and give his own name to the Romans. For them I have set no limit of time or space. To them I grant power without end. Indeed, even the stern goddess Juno, who is troubling and alarming the sea, the earth and the sky, will change her plans for the better, and join me in helping the Romans to become, first, masters of the world, then a nation of peace. This is my will: a time will come as the years slip by when these descendants of Troy will enslave the homes of the Greeks who sacked Troy, and lord it over their conquered cities!

'Then shall a Caesar[14] be born, of fine Trojan stock, Julius, a name derived from the great Iulus; his dominion will reach to the Ocean, his fame to the stars. And when he comes back from the East, laden with spoil, you will, never fear, welcome him to the heavens; and men will pray to him too. After him the age of violence will soften, and there will be no more wars. Old-fashioned Loyalty, Home, Remus and Romulus gone to join the gods, shall make the laws. The iron-bound, grim gates of war shall be shut upon godless Madness, squatting inside on the cruel weapons of war: a hundred knots of bronze shall bind its arms behind its back, for all the hideous howling from its bloodied lips.'

297–304   Jupiter makes sure that Dido, queen of Carthage, welcomes the Trojan survivors.

With these words Jupiter sends Mercury[15] down from on high to ensure that the land and new-built towers of Carthage shall welcome the Trojans, in case Queen Dido, unaware of Fate, should turn them away. Through the depths of space he flies on the beat of his wings, and swiftly lands on the shores of Libya. Obediently he softens the stern Carthaginian hearts, as Jupiter wills, inspiring the queen above all with feelings of peace and kindness towards the Trojans.

305–34   Aeneas sets out to reconnoitre and meets his mother, disguised as a young huntress: he asks her about the country they have come to.

However, the steadfast Aeneas spent the night worrying over his many problems, and as soon as the kind light of day allowed, he determined to set out and explore this strange country, to find out where the wind had brought them, and whether men or – so desolate did it look – only wild animals lived there, then to report back to his men. (He had hidden his fleet right under the overhang of a cliff, camouflaged by trees which cast a spooky half-light.) He strode off with Achates, no one else, with a pair of iron-tipped spears quivering in his hand.

In the middle of the wood he was met by his mother, who had put on the looks, dress and weapons of a Spartan girl, or of an Amazon who could outlast horses, outsprint the swiftest of rivers. Just like a huntress she had a bow handy, slung over her shoulders, and had tied the full skirt of her dress up, baring her knees, leaving her hair to blow loose in the wind. She was the first to speak: 'Hallo there, sirs, please tell me, have you perhaps seen one of my sisters, roaming about here – she was wearing a quiver and a spotted lynx-skin cloak – or else in full cry after a boar with foam-flecked jaws?'

So spoke Venus, and Venus' son replied: 'No sight or sound of your sister. But, maiden, what am I to call you? For your face is no mortal's, no more is your voice; you must be a goddess – Apollo's sister? One of the Nymphs? – be kind, whoever you are

19

and relieve our anxiety: tell us where in the world we are, what shores we've been forced to land on. We've been driven off course by the wind and huge waves; we know nothing of this place or its people. Tell us, and victim after victim will fall to my hand at your altar.'

335–85 The 'huntress' tells Aeneas where he is, and relates the story of Dido.

Then Venus said: 'I deserve no such honour; all Tyrian girls wear a quiver and high scarlet hunting-boots like these. The kingdom you see is Phoenician, the people migrated from Tyre, the city is Carthage – but the country belongs to the Libyans, a people not to be tackled in war. Queen Dido rules here – she left Tyre to escape her brother. The tale of the wrong he did her is a long one, long and involved: I'll just tell you the gist of it. She had a husband, Sychaeus, the richest of all the Phoenicians, devotedly loved by the poor woman whose father had given her to him, a virgin bride, in due ceremonial marriage. King of Tyre was her brother Pygmalion, a monster of crime without equal. An act of sheer madness came between them. Blinded by lust for gold, the godless Pygmalion showed not the slightest regard for his sister's love for Sychaeus: he stealthily cut him down, off guard in front of the altar. For a long time he kept the crime hidden, evilly fobbing her off with lie after lie, cheating the love-sick Dido with empty hopes. But then the ghost of her unburied husband came to her in a dream, eerily raising before her its bloodless face. It disclosed the atrocious deed at the altar, the sword wound in its breast, and exposed the whole crime in the family. It urged her, then, to escape from the country in haste, revealing, to help her journey, the secret of old buried treasure, an unknown hoard of silver and gold.

'Horrified, Dido began to arrange the escape with her friends. Getting together all those who bitterly hated the tyrant, or feared him, they seized some ships which chanced to be ready for sea, and carried the gold on board. So the wealth of the greedy Pygmalion was hurried away overseas. The woman it was that led them. They came to the place where soon you will see rising the great walls and fortress of a new city, Carthage. They bought the land, "as much as the hide of a bull could surround", and so call it Bull's Hide.[16]

'But who, please, are you? What land have you come from? And where are you making for?'

And Aeneas, sighing, drawing his voice from the depths of his soul, answered her queries: 'Goddess, if I tell you everything right from the start, if you have time to listen to the tedious tale of our woes, evening will fall on Olympus before I am finished.

'Sailing from ancient Troy – perhaps you have heard of Troy? – we were driven off course by the whim of a storm to Libya's shores. I am dutiful Aeneas, and I have on board with me the gods of our homeland, which I saved from the enemy. I am, you see, famous in heaven and beyond. Yet, descended from almighty Jupiter though I am, I'm searching for Italy to make it my fatherland. With a fleet of twenty ships I sailed out over the Phrygian sea, and my mother, a goddess, was pointing the way as I followed my promised destiny. But ripped apart by the wind and sea, barely seven of the ships survive. And I am a nobody, helpless, wandering the deserts of Africa, banished from Europe and Asia, the whole civilised world.'

386–401   Venus interrupts Aeneas, and heads him towards Dido's palace, where he will rejoin his lost companions.

Venus could bear his distress no longer, and broke in on his grief. 'Whoever you are, you cannot, I'm sure, be hated by heaven; you're alive and breathing, and you've come to a Tyrian city. Just carry straight on, go right to the palace. For here's news for you: your comrades are back, the fleet has returned, all driven to safety by a shift in the wind – unless, that is, all that my parents taught me of reading the bird-signs is wrong. Look! See those twelve swans flying in joyful formation – a moment ago an eagle, King Jupiter's bird, swooped down and scattered them over the sky, but now, in a long line, they seem to be making for land, looking down at those that have landed already! They are flocking together in play, now they're back, slapping their wings, circling the sky in a group, making their song! In the same way your ships and your young warriors have, some of them, made it to port already, and others are under full sail, just coming to harbour. Just keep straight on, follow the path where it leads.'

402–29   Venus now reveals herself in all her beauty, and floats away to her home, leaving Aeneas and Achates wrapped in mist.

Venus stopped speaking, and as she turned away her neck glowed rose-pink, and a heavenly fragrance breathed from the glorious hair on her head. Her dress flowed down now, full to her feet, and the majesty of her walk made it clear that she was truly a goddess. Aeneas, recognising his mother, sent his words chasing after her as she vanished: 'Why do you too mock me like this, cruelly fooling your son with illusions? Why may we not join hands, and speak truly, face to face?' With this cry of reproach he strode off to the city.

But as Aeneas and Achates went they were shrouded darkly in mist, as the goddess cloaked them thickly in cloud, so that no one might see or touch them, try to get in their way, or ask why they came. Then she winged her way happily home, back to her favourite haunt in Paphos,[17] for there stood her temple and her hundred altars, alight with Arabian incense and the scent of fresh flowers.

Meanwhile the two pressed on where the path led, and soon were climbing the long line of a hill which loomed over the city, with a view straight down on the citadel. Aeneas marvels at the massive buildings, where huts had recently stood, marvels at the gates and the noise from the stone-paved streets. The Tyrians are working at a blistering rate – some of them laying long walls and laboriously building the citadel, rolling up the stones by hand, others choosing the site for a house, marking it out with a trench. Here they are dredging a harbour, here laying deep foundations for a theatre, and quarrying great columns of stone to add grace to its stage. They are making their laws, and choosing officials of state to rule them.

430–40   Virgil likes to illuminate his work with *similes* – sharply observed comparisons often, as here, drawn from nature.

This is how on a sunny day in the spring, bees toil away in the fields of flowers, when they lead the young bees out, or pack the combs full of oozing honey, bulging the cells with its sweetness. Some of them take over the loads from the incoming workers, while some form an army to drive off the work-shy drones from the hive. There's a buzz of activity, and the honey is fragrant with thyme.

'What fortunate people, *their* city's already half built!' says Aeneas, peering up at the roof-tops. Then, still shrouded in mist – miraculously – he moves into their midst and joins them, but not one of them sees him.

441–93   Aeneas and Achates find an open space, with some trees still standing, in the centre of the new city. Aeneas waits here, perhaps aware that the queen is bound to come to this focal point of the city's activities. Here on the walls of a temple being built in honour of Juno are painted scenes from the Trojan War. And here, where he sees Dido's hopes coming true, he dares for the first time to hope that he too may be successful.

494–519   While Aeneas and Achates, still invisible, are wondering at the pictures, Dido enters the temple. Then Aeneas catches sight of some of his lost companions.

While Aeneas was standing in awe, gazing spellbound and lost in these marvellous pictures, Queen Dido, beautiful beyond comparison, entered the temple, a great troop of young warriors around her, Now, when the goddess Diana dances along the banks of her river, or down the slopes of a favourite mountain, attended by a throng of mountain nymphs, with her quiver over her shoulder, there's no other goddess to match her in height or grace as she runs, and the heart of her mother Latona is seized with a joy beyond words. Just like her, Queen Dido was happily moving through the courtiers to urge on the work, to hasten her future realm. Then, under the vault at the heart of Juno's temple, close by the holy doors and shielded by the spears of her guards, she sat down, leaning back in her throne on high. She began to dispense laws to her people, and justice, assigning the various duties fairly, or sharing them out by lot.

Suddenly Aeneas saw Antheus approaching through the crowd, and Sergestus with brave Cloanthus and some more of the Trojans, those whom the black whirlwind had scattered all over the sea and driven far off down the coast. Aeneas and Achates were stunned to see them, shaken by joy and anxiety mixed, and fired with a desire to clasp their hands, yet confused by the puzzle of events. They kept out of sight, still cloaked in their shroud of mist, watching to discover what had happened, where they had beached their ships, and why they had come. Spokesmen from all the ships kept arriving, noisily heading for the temple to ask for the queen's indulgence.

520–60   One of the Trojan survivors identifies himself and his companions as devoted followers of Aeneas, and asks to be allowed to repair their ships and go on their way. His speech serves both to tell the reader what has been happening, and to make Dido aware of how much the Trojans admire Aeneas.

They entered, were given permission to speak, and the oldest, Ilioneus, calmly began.

'Your majesty, Jupiter gave you leave to found a new city and to restrain proud tribes with the bridle of justice: we poor Trojans, storm-driven over the seas, beg you, stop your men from the monstrous crime of burning our ships. We're a god-fearing people; spare us, and give a kind thought instead to our plight. We've not come to plunder your Libyan homes, or to carry loot down to the beaches. We've no mind for violence – we're victims, not victors.

'There's a place which the Greeks call Westland; it is ancient and powerful, with fertile soil. The people of Italus lived there: their descendants now, so the story goes, call themselves after their leader, Italians. That's where we were sailing to, when suddenly the storm-star Orion, rising with mountainous waves drove us on unseen shoals, and the south wind wildly, viciously, scattered our ships through the surge and unbroken reefs, whipping the surf mast-high. We, just a few of us, have splashed our way here to your shores.

'What sort of men are these? What barbarous country is this that allows such customs? We're not even allowed to rest on the sand; they threaten to fight, and bar us even from setting foot on dry land. You may care nothing for human beings or the weapons of men, but think of the gods; they never forget good deeds or bad. Our king was Aeneas; no man has been more just or dutiful, no one greater in war and fighting. If Fate still keeps him alive, if he breathes the air of heaven, and does not yet sleep in death's cruel darkness, then we have no cause for fear, nor will you regret being first to help us. And in Sicily we have cities to support us, and King Acestes, sprung of Trojan blood. Let us but beach our storm-broken fleet, and shape new timbers in the woods and cut oars from branches, so that we may happily make our way to Italy and Latium – if destiny will let us find our friends and king, and head for Italy.

'But if our hopes are lost, and the Libyan sea has closed over the prince of Troy, if all hope for Iulus, too, is gone, then let us sail for Sicily at least, the last land we touched at, and for the homes that are there ready for us, and call Acestes king.'

561–78   So said Ilioneus, and every Trojan throat roared agreement. Dido promises to help the Trojans on their way, but opens her city to them if they care to stay. She will send a search party after Aeneas.

Then Dido, eyes lowered, spoke briefly: 'Banish all fear and worry from your hearts, Trojans. My position here is difficult, and my city is young: that's why I have to do such things, and guard every inch of my frontiers. But who has not heard of Aeneas' men, of the city of Troy, the courage of its heroes, and the fires of its awful wars? Our Carthaginian wits are not as dull as that, nor is our city so cut off from the rest of the world! Whether you choose the great Westland, or Sicily, where Trojan Acestes is king, I'll send you safely on your way, and help with men and provisions. Or do you wish to settle here with me, and share my kingdom? This city I'm building, it's yours. Haul up your ships. Trojan or Tyrian, I'll treat you the same. And how I wish the same south wind had driven King Aeneas here! I'll send trusty men down the coast, and tell them to search the furthest corners of the country, in case he's been cast ashore and is lost in some forest or city.'

579–612   The mist round Aeneas and Achates suddenly disappears. Aeneas greets Dido, promising never to forget her.

Emboldened by her words brave Achates and Aeneas, leader of his people, had for some time been keen to dispel the mist. But first Achates addressed Aeneas.

'Son of Venus, have you made up your mind what to do? Everything's safe, as you see, our fleet and friends are back with us. Only one is missing, and we saw him drowned in the middle of the storm. Everything else matches what your mother said.'

He'd hardly spoken when the mist surrounding them cleared suddenly and melted into pure clean air. There stood Aeneas, his head and shoulders radiant in the bright light: his mother Venus herself had breathed grace into her son's hair, the bright flush of youth into his cheeks, and the light of happiness into his eyes. In the same way is ivory given beauty by the hand of the artist, and silver or marble by a lustrous setting of gold.

So then he addressed the queen, suddenly appearing to everyone's amazement, and said: 'Here, the man you are looking for, Aeneas of Troy, here I am, saved from the Libyan waves. My lady, no one but you has felt any pity for Troy's terrible anguish! We are the few left alive by the Greeks, exhausted by all our disasters on land and sea; we've nothing – yet you offer a share in your city, your home! We've no means of repaying your kindness, Dido, none of the Trojans has, wherever they are, scattered all over the world. But if ever the powers above take note of the goodness of men, if there's any justice at all, anywhere, any innate notion of right, may the gods grant you the reward you deserve. What golden age were you born in? What great parents produced such a daughter? As long as the rivers run down to the seas, as long as the shadows sweep over the slopes of the mountains, and the sky keeps the stars alight, your name shall live for ever in honour and praise, no matter what land I am called to.'

When he'd spoken he stretched out a hand to his friend Ilioneus, and one to Serestus, then to the rest, brave Gyas and brave Cloanthus.

613–42   Dido welcomes Aeneas, and prepares a splendid reception for him in the palace.

Queen Dido was dumbfounded at her first sight of the hero and the thought of his terrible misfortunes, but then found words.

'What ill luck drives you, the son of a goddess, through such fearful dangers? What power has brought you to these inhospitable shores? Are you really the Aeneas whom gentle Venus bore to Trojan Anchises, by the banks of the river of Troy? I well remember Teucer[18] coming to Tyre: he was in exile from his homeland Salamis, and in search of a new land to be king of, with the help of my father Belus, for Belus was then sacking Cyprus and keeping it under control. From that time I have known of the fall of Troy, known your name and the names of the kings of the Greeks. So please, sirs, come into my home. I too suffered untold hardships like yours, till Fortune allowed me to settle at last in this land – I am well schooled in misfortune, and this is my first lesson in helping the unlucky.'

With these words she took Aeneas to the royal palace, and ordered thanksgiving to be paid to the gods in their temples. At the same time she sent twenty bulls to his companions down by the shore, a hundred huge bristly-backed swine, the same number of ewes and fat lambs, and gifts of wine to delight them. Inside, the palace was being decked out in the glitter of regal splendour, and a banquet was laid in the hall; there were tapestries skilfully worked in proud scarlet thread, on the tables a great service of silver, with the noble deeds of Dido's forebears in golden relief, the full tale of their history traced through the long line of her family's heroes right from the ancient beginnings of her race.

643–56   Aeneas sends Achates to the ships to fetch Ascanius, and gifts for Dido.

But Aeneas' love for his son would allow him no peace, so he sends Achates running to the ships, to take the news to Ascanius, and to bring back the boy: all his concern as a father is fixed on his dear son Ascanius. Moreover he bids him fetch some gifts snatched from the ruins of Troy, a cloak stiff with figures embroidered in gold, a dress with a floral border of bright yellow, once worn by Queen Helen, who took it with her from Sparta on her way to Troy and that unlawful 'marriage' with Paris, a wonderful gift from Leda, her mother. In addition a sceptre once carried by Ilione, the eldest daughter of King Priam, a necklace of pearls and a double tiara of jewels and gold. Off went Achates, hurrying down to the ships on his mission.

657–94   Venus plots to make Dido fall in love with Aeneas,
telling her son Cupid to impersonate Ascanius.

Venus now devises a cunning new scheme, to let Cupid, by
assuming his looks, take the place of the charming Ascanius;
with the gifts he must kindle the queen to passion, envelop her
innermost being in love's flames. In truth she's afraid of the
palace welcome, of Tyrian double-talk. She frets at Juno's
hostility, and her worries flood back as the evening advances.
So she turns to her winged son Cupid, and says: 'My son, you
are all my strength, all the power that is mine; you alone, my
son, can laugh at Jove and his thunderbolts; I come to you for
help, and beg your divine favour. Your brother Aeneas, racked
by storms, is driven from shore to shore through Juno's bitter
hostility: these facts you know, often you've shared my grief at
them. But now that Tyrian woman, Dido, keeps him, delays him
with flattering words, and I don't trust her welcome – Juno's
behind it, she won't be idle when so much depends on it. So I'm
planning to get to the queen first by a trick, to enslave her with
passion, so that once her great love for Aeneas has bound her to
me, no god can change her. Now here's my plan, listen to how
you can manage it.

'Aeneas has sent for his dear son – he's a darling boy to me too
– and the young prince is about to set off for the palace, taking
the gifts that survived the great fires of Troy and the sea. I shall
hide him away, drugged in sleep, in one of my holy places, in
case he should find out my plans, or blunder right into the
middle of things. You, for one night, no more, must cunningly
impersonate him, you're both boys, and put on his familiar
features, so that when Dido joyfully sits you on her lap, even at
the height of the banquet with the wine still flowing, hugging you
close and raining sweet kisses upon you, you may secretly
breathe passion into her, and slip her the poison of love.'

Then Cupid obeys his beloved mother's commands, takes off
his wings, and gleefully strides off in the walk of Ascanius. Venus
pours soothing sleep over Ascanius' limbs, and herself flies off
with him safe and snug in her arms to lofty groves in the East,
where soft marjoram beds him down in the flowers and sweet-
scented shade.

Now, obedient to his mother's wishes, Cupid was cheerfully on his way at the side of Achates, taking the royal gifts to the palace. As he arrives the queen has taken her place beneath magnificent tapestries, on her golden couch set in the middle of the company. Aeneas and his Trojans have arrived, and recline on the purple-covered couches. Servants offer them water for their hands, serve bread from baskets and hand them the fine woollen napkins. There are fifty maidservants in the kitchen, whose job it is, in due turn, to keep the larder well stocked with provisions, or to build up the fires in the hearths. Another hundred maidservants are there, and a hundred menservants too, all young, to set out the wine-cups, and bring the food to the tables.

The Carthaginians too have arrived, flocking into the festive hall of the palace. All the guests on their bright-coloured couches are admiring Aeneas' gifts and Aeneas' son – or rather, they're admiring Cupid's glowing good looks, and false conversation – the cloak, and the dress with its yellow floral border. But most of all Dido, poor Dido, doomed to a ruinous love, can't gaze enough, and falls even more deeply in love as she gazes, equally moved by the boy and the gifts. As for Cupid, he put his arms round Aeneas' neck, kissed him and clung to him, indulging the great love of his 'father' – then turns to the queen. Her heart and her eyes enfold him, and fondly she hugs him again and again to her breast, unaware, poor thing, of the power of the god that possesses her. And Cupid, remembering his mother's instructions, begins step by step to blot out her love for Sychaeus, tries to put in its place, into her desolate heart so long out of practice, a love that's alive.

At the first pause in the banquet the table is cleared, and great garlanded bowls of sweet wine are brought in. The noise swells in the hall as their voices roll up to the rafters. There are lamps hanging down from the gold-panelled ceiling; their light and the blaze of the torches banish the darkness. Then the queen calls for the heavy gold gem-studded vessel that King Belus and all his descendants had used, and fills it with wine, just as they had. In the silence that follows she prays: 'Jupiter, for you, so they say, make the laws for both guest and host, make this day happy for us Tyrians, and for these folk who set out from Troy – a day for our children to remember. May Bacchus, giver of joy, be present, and kindly Juno. And you too, my people, all of you, favour this feast with your good will and blessing.'

736–47   As the wine is passed from hand to hand, the guests are entertained with a song about the wonders of the universe.

748–56   And far into the night poor Dido talks of many things, drinking down deep draughts of love; she asks question after question, about Priam and Hector: 'What arms,' she said, 'did Memnon come with – what were the horses of Diomede like – how tall was Achilles? No! Tell us, dear guest, the whole tale right from the start, the cunning of the Greeks, the deaths of your comrades, your own wanderings. For you have been wandering, over the lands and the seas of the world, for seven years.'

Notes to Book I

1 **Fate**   In Latin *fatum*, what is spoken. Fate is what is laid down as destiny, the will of the gods. It is also identified with the Fates, three daughters of Night, who spin men's destiny. Although the fate of an individual may be altered, Fate, or the Fates, can never be changed or overruled.
2 **Samos**   An island in the Aegean Sea; it had a famous temple of Juno.
3 **Ganymede**   Mythological Trojan boy-prince, carried off to heaven to be Jupiter's cup-bearer.
4 **Cassandra**   After Troy's capture, Ajax son of Oileus dragged Priam's daughter Cassandra away from the image of Athena where she had sought refuge, and raped her.
5 **Nymphs**   Fairy-like young semi-goddesses.
6 **Diomede**   A great Greek warrior.
7 **Sarpedon**   The best warrior among Troy's allies, killed by Patroclus.
8 **Orontes**   Like Sarpedon, one of Troy's allies from Lycia, in south-west Turkey.
9 **Antheus, Capys, Caicus**   Trojan ship-captains, comrades of Aeneas.
10 **Acestes**   King of part of Sicily, of Trojan descent.
11 **Scylla**   A monster which seized and devoured mariners who sailed near

its cave, which overlooked the straits between Sicily and Italy, with the whirlpool of Charybdis opposite it.

12 **Cyclops** A one-eyed giant living in Sicily. (His story is in Book III.)

13 **Orontes . . . Amycus . . . Lycus . . . Gyas . . . Cloanthus** All comrades of Aeneas, supposedly lost at sea in the storm.

14 **Caesar** Probably Julius Caesar, though Virgil may mean Augustus Caesar, who succeeded Julius as the first emperor of Rome. However all the remarks which follow the words 'After him the age of violence. . .' refer to Augustus.

15 **Mercury (Hermes)** A god who acted as Jupiter's messenger.

16 **Bull's Hide** In Latin, Byrsa = bull's hide: the legend is that the hide was cut into one very long thin strip, and it is thought that Byrsa was the Carthaginian name for the citadel of their city.

17 **Paphos** A town in Cyprus where Venus was especially worshipped: according to legend Venus emerged from the sea at birth, and first came to land at Paphos.

18 **Teucer** The story is that the Greek Teucer, after returning home to Salamis after the Trojan War, was forced to leave home and found a new Salamis in Cyprus, because he was thought responsible for the death of his brother Ajax, son of Telamon. Virgil uses the legend to explain how Dido should have heard of Aeneas.

Book II

Aeneas begins his story. He explains how the Trojans were tricked into taking the Wooden Horse into Troy, instead of listening to Laocoon, the priest of Neptune, who begs them to destroy it. He relates the horrifying death of Laocoon. Aeneas then in a dream sees Hector, one of the king's sons killed earlier in the war, who warns him to save himself, the Trojan people, and their gods. Aeneas wakes up to find that the Greeks have broken into the city, and plunges into the fighting. He sees King Priam brutally slaughtered by Achilles' son Pyrrhus. As he is about to kill Helen in revenge, Athena stops him: she reveals that nothing can now save Troy as the gods have joined in the destruction of the city, and persuades him to escape. His father Anchises at first refuses to leave his beloved home, but is finally persuaded, and Aeneas leads his family and some other followers out of the burning city. But on the way his wife, Creusa, is lost, and Aeneas dashes madly back into the confusion to find her. His search is interrupted by her ghost, which tells him his destiny, and persuades him to return to the rest of his family. The refugees assemble on Mount Ida.

❧❧❧❧❧

Book II is the first half of a long flashback, in which we learn how Troy was taken by the Greeks (the first full account in the literature of Greece or Rome). Aeneas is the true heroic warrior, ready to brave any danger in defence of his country, ready to die when all is lost. Gradually he learns that he has new responsibilities, that death is too easy an escape from his troubles. Yet he forgets all the divine warnings and prophecies when he charges back into the ruins of Troy in search of his lost wife. It is only her ghost that finally convinces him that his world is gone for ever, and that he must lead the struggle to build a new life out of its ruins.

Characters

Gods

Athena, also known as Pallas Athene and, by the Romans, as Minerva: daughter of Jupiter, patron goddess of Greek cities and all handicrafts

Venus
Apollo, god of prophecy
Neptune

Trojans
Aeneas
Creusa, his wife
Anchises, his father
Ascanius, his son (also known as Iulus)
Laocoon, priest of Neptune, and Aeneas' uncle
Priam, king of Troy
Hecuba, his wife
Cassandra, his daughter
Hector and Paris, his sons, already killed in the war at this time
Panthus, priest of Apollo
Coroebus, in love with Cassandra

Greeks
Agamemnon, king of Mycenae, leader of the Greek expedition to
    Troy
Achilles and Diomede, famous fighters
Ulysses, also called Odysseus by the Greeks, inventor of the
    Wooden Horse
Pyrrhus, also called Neoptolemus, son of Achilles
Sinon, a Greek agent
Calchas, a Greek prophet

 1–20   Aeneas begins reluctantly to explain to Dido and her
guests why the Greeks built the Wooden Horse.

All fell silent, their faces rapt in attention. From his place at the
head of the table Prince Aeneas started to speak: 'The sorrows
you bid me relive are quite beyond words – the destruction by
the Greeks of the rich but pitiful kingdom of Troy, all the tragic
events that I saw and took a great part in myself. No soldier who
served under Achilles or his son or stubborn Ulysses could ever
hold back his tears in telling this sad story. And already the
misty night is tumbling down from the sky, already the setting
stars invite us to rest. But if you are really so filled with desire to
learn our misfortunes and hear a brief tale of the death-throes of

33

Troy, even though I shudder at the memory and recoil from the pain, I will try.

'Broken in battle, and baffled by Fate as year after year slipped away, the Greek commanders, thanks to Athena's divine skills, built a horse the size of a mountain, with pine planks interlaced for its ribs. They pretended it was an offering to make sure of their safe return home – that's the story they spread. Drawing lots for their places, they secretly concealed in the dark of the horse's belly specially selected men, packing the great cavernous womb full with a squad of armed soldiers.'

21–39   The Greeks sail away. The Trojans find the horse by the shore, and wonder what to do with it.

'In sight of the land there's the well-known island of Tenedos, rich and powerful while Priam was king, but now little more than a curving, treacherous anchorage: here the Greeks sailed, and hid on its empty shore. Gone! we thought – shipping back on the wind to Mycenae! All of us flung off the fetters of grief we had worn so long. The gates flew open: what fun it was, going down to their camp, not a soul in sight, the whole beach deserted! Here were the tents of cruel Achilles, here were his son's! There was the place for the ships! That's where we fought them! Some of us gazed spellbound at the deadly gift of the maiden Athena, staggered by the size of the Horse. Thymoetes was the first to urge us to drag it inside the walls, to set it up in the citadel. Was he a traitor? – or perhaps Troy's fate was now being sealed. But Capys, together with all those who took a more sensible view, suspected the gift was a trick of the Greeks and a trap, and told us to hurl it into the sea, or light a fire under it; or else to bore holes in the belly, and probe the inside of it. The people were split into two camps, undecided which course of action to support.'

40–56   The discussion is interrupted by Laocoon, the priest of Neptune, who rushes down from the citadel to scold the Trojans for their stupidity.

'Then a huge mob came running down from the citadel with Laocoon, blazing with anger, in front of them all. From far off he yelled: "Citizens, poor fools, are you mad? Do you believe the enemy's gone? Do you think any gift of the Greeks is free of deceit? Is that typical of Ulysses? There are Greeks concealed behind all this wood – or it's a contraption designed to destroy our walls, to spy into our homes, to swoop down on our city! There's trickery of some sort lurking here. Don't trust the Horse, fellow-Trojans. Whatever it is, I'm afraid of the Greeks, even when they're offering gifts!"

'So he spoke, and with all his strength he rifled his mighty spear into the Horse's side, the curving frame of its belly. It stuck there, quivering, and the womb resounded as its cavernous hollows echoed and groaned. But the gods were against us, our minds were closed to the truth – otherwise he'd have forced us to make a shambles of that hiding-place of the Greeks with our swords, and the city of Troy, Priam's tall citadel, would still be standing.'

57–75   Suddenly a prisoner is dragged in – but he's not what he seems!

'And then they caught sight of a man, with his hands bound behind him; some Trojan shepherds were hauling him noisily up to the king: the stranger had come up and surrendered to them of his own accord, for just this purpose, to lay Troy open to the Greeks. He put his trust in his wits, ready to succeed in his schemes or to face certain death if he failed. The young Trojans came pouring round him, eager to stare at the prisoner, outdoing each other in mocking him. Hear how the Greeks deceived us, learn what they are all like from this one man's villainy!

'He stood there with all eyes upon him, confused and defenceless, peering round at the army of us Trojans. "Help! Is there any land left, any sea that will take me? What remains for me now at the end of my misery, when I can't go back to the Greeks anywhere, and the Trojans are enemies too, and after my blood?"

'At this pitiful cry of anguish our feelings changed and our violent anger abated. We urged him to say who he was, what he could tell us, and to explain what he was up to in letting himself be captured.'

77–104   Sinon relates how he was persecuted by Ulysses after boasting that he would avenge his friend Palamedes.

'"I'll tell you the whole truth, Your Majesty, whatever it costs; first of all, I shall not deny I'm a Greek – misfortune may ruin poor Sinon, it shall not maliciously make me a liar as well! Some talk has come to your ears, perhaps, of famed Palamedes – you've heard of his glorious name? – the Greeks falsely and foully framed him on charges of high treason because he spoke up against war, and, though he was innocent, put him to death; now they're sorry he's dead. Well, I was related to him, and since we were poor my father had sent me, young though I was, to serve as his squire. While he was still a power in the kingdom, still one of the king's influential advisers, I too enjoyed something of his name and reputation. But when he had left the land of the living – the plausible lies of Ulysses killed him, the story's well known – I was ruined, and dragged out a miserable life in the shadows, bitterly angry at the fate of my innocent friend. Like a fool I couldn't keep quiet: if ever we won and returned home to Argos, I vowed, then, given the chance, I'd avenge him. These words aroused fierce hatred. That was the start of my downfall. From then on Ulysses kept spreading alarm with fresh accusations, kept dropping slanderous hints and stirring up plots against me. Nor did he stop till with the help of Calchas – but why do I harp on these unwelcome facts? There's no point in it; why waste your time if you think all the Greeks are the same, if to hear the name 'Greek' is enough? Punish me now, as you've long since decided – that's what Ulysses would want, Agamemnon would pay gladly to hear it, and Menelaus."'

105–44   Sinon's pretended despair makes the Trojans more eager to find out 'the facts'. He explains how he was chosen as a sacrifice to ensure good weather for the Greeks' journey home, and how he escaped.

'Then of course we were even more anxious to find out the rest of the story – we had no idea of the Greeks, how evil and cunning they are. He continued, trembling, and spoke as if from the heart.

'"Often the Greeks, exhausted by the length of the war, longed to abandon it, to leave Troy behind and make their way home. How I wish they had done so! But rough weather at sea always prevented them, head winds scared them from sailing. And when this Horse had been built of its maple planks and stood ready, then even more did the whole sky rumble with thunderstorms. In this deadlock we sent Eurypylus to enquire of Apollo's oracle, and he came back with this grim answer; 'With the blood of the maiden, Iphigenia, you appeased the winds when you first set sail for Troy; with blood, the blood of a Greek, you must pay for your journey home.' When these words reached the ears of the people they were stunned, and an icy tremor of fear ran through their bones – who was it they were to kill, whom did Apollo demand?

'"Then with a great uproar Ulysses dragged out Calchas the prophet into the open, demanding to know the will of the gods. Already many of them were guessing that I was the intended victim of that schemer's cruel plot, and saw what would happen – but said not a word.

'"For ten days Calchas was silent and stayed in his tent, refusing to name anyone, and so condemn him to death. But at last, giving way, as they'd planned, to Ulysses' ranting insistence, he broke silence, and sentenced me to the altar. There was unanimous approval: what each man had feared for himself he was happy to accept if it meant that some other poor wretch was to die. The dreadful day came; the instruments of sacrifice, the sacred salt meal[1] and the headband were made ready for the victim – me. Then, I confess, I escaped from my fate, broke my bonds and lay hid through the night, concealed in the mud and the reeds of a lake, hoping against hope that they'd sail.

'"Now I have given up all expectation of seeing my own country again, the children I love or the father I long for: the Greeks, perhaps, will demand retribution from them for my escape, and kill them, poor wretches, to atone for my crime. So now I beg you, by the gods above, by the guardians of Truth, by Trust, if Trust survives unbroken anywhere among men, pity my sufferings, pity me for my undeserved hardships."'

145–98   The Trojans spare Sinon's life. When Priam asks why the Horse was built Sinon explains that it is a holy offering to Athena – if the Trojans destroy it they will destroy Troy; if they take it safe into Troy they will destroy the Greeks.

'For these tears we grant him his life, and even feel sorry for him. Priam himself at once orders him to be freed from his fetters and chains, and talks to him kind-heartedly: "Whoever you are, forget the Greeks; you're free from them now. Become one of us, and answer me truly. Why did they build the enormous bulk of the Horse? Who thought of it? What is its purpose? Is it some gift to the gods, or an engine of war?"

'And Sinon, skilled in deceit and the craft of the Greeks, lifted his hands, freed of chains, to the stars: "Sun and Moon, eternal fires of heaven, invincible powers, I call you to witness, and you altars, and the murderous knife which I fled from, and the head-band I wore as a victim: it's no crime to break the vows which I swore as a Greek, it's no crime to hate those people or to disclose all their secrets; I'm no longer bound by the laws of my country. If I tell the truth, sir, and amply repay your kindness, then stand by your word as a Trojan; if I keep you safe, keep faith with me.

'"All the hopes of the Greeks, their confidence in starting the war, were based on the help of Athena. But from the moment the godless Diomede,² and Ulysses, inventor of crimes, crept up to your citadel, killed the guards and stole from its holy temple Troy's fateful statue of Athena, when they snatched up that sacred image and dared to lay bloodstained hands on the goddess's virginal headband – from that moment the tide of Greek hopes ebbed away, their strength was broken, the goddess herself turned against them. There was no shadow of doubt in the warning signs she gave us. The statue had hardly been set up in our camp, when fire flickered and flashed from its blazing eyes, a salt sweat ran over its limbs, and three times, miraculous-ly, with its shield and quivering spear, it leapt up of its own accord.

'" At once Calchas told us what it meant. We must dare the seas: Troy could not fall to our spears till we'd asked Athena's favour again, in our homeland, and brought back her blessing. (They came with it over the sea in their sleek curved ships; now they've gone back to Mycenae to fetch fresh forces, and to seek the gods' favour again – then they'll be back over the seas – unexpectedly.) That's what, said Calchas, the omens meant. That's why they built this copy of a horse, to atone for the theft of the statue and the insult to the goddess, to cleanse their awful guilt. In fact Calchas told them to make it this enormous size, rising sky high with its timber planks, so that it couldn't be brought through the gates and inside the walls, thereby transferring its ancient protection to you. If your hands defiled this gift to Athena, then massive destruction would fall on Priam's kingdom and people; (may the gods let it fall first on Calchas!). But if your hands were to help it climb right up into your city, then Asia would mount an invasion into the cities of Greece; that was the fate in store for our children's children."

'That's how the cunning and skill of the lying Sinon led us to believe him. We were hoodwinked by his wiles and feigned tears, we whom Diomede, Ulysses, ten years' war and a thousand ships had not been able to beat!'

199–227   The Trojans are finally convinced by a dreadful sight. Laocoon, while sacrificing to Neptune, is attacked by two sea-serpents, which disappear into Athena's temple after devouring the priest and his two sons.

'Then, poor unsuspecting souls that we were, we saw something even more dreadful that muddled our minds still further. Laocoon had been chosen by lot as the priest of Neptune: he was sacrificing a great bull at the ceremonial altar, when suddenly over the deep calm sea from Tenedos – I shudder to recall it – two serpents, with their great coils breasting the surface, came swimming side by side to the shore. Their necks towered over the water, their crests, blood-red, topped the waves; the rest of their serpentine bodies slithered over the surface behind them, writhing and rolling. The salt spume hissed: and now they were just about landing, their eyeballs blazing and bloodshot, their forked tongues flickering fire.

'We went pale at the sight, and scattered. The serpents charged straight at Laocoon: each of them first seized one of his little sons, twining its coils round his body, then bit off and swallowed the poor child's limbs. Laocoon snatched a sword, dashed to help: but they seized him, binding their great spirals about him. Twice round his waist wound their scaly length, twice round his throat, their heads and necks still looming over him. All the time he was straining to tear off their knots with his hands, his headbands drenched in their blood and dark venom. His terrible screams floated to heaven, like the bellowing of a wounded bull which bolts from the altar and shakes off the ill-aimed axe from its neck. But the serpents glided away, up to the shrine of cruel Athena high on the citadel, and vanished under the circular shield at her feet.'

228–49   Laocoon's attempt to persuade the Trojans to destroy the Horse had been foiled by Sinon's appearance; now his death scares them into believing that he has been punished for attacking the Horse, so they drag it into Troy, and start celebrating.

'Then a fresh panic assailed their terrified hearts; no one doubted that Laocoon had been properly punished for the crime of hurling his wicked spear at the Horse's flank, and profaning the sacred timbers. "We must take this holy image to the altar," they cried, "and pray for Athena's good will."

'We broke a way through the walls, and opened the city's defences. Everyone joined in the work, putting rollers under its hooves, stretching cables up to its neck. The deadly machine climbed over our walls, pregnant with death. Young boys and girls accompanied its progress with hymns, and rejoiced to lay hands on the cable. On it came, and glided threateningly into the heart of our city.

'O my country, O Troy, home of the gods, whose walls are so famed in war! Four times it stopped, right in the gateway, and every time the clang of their weapons rang out from its womb. But we paid no attention, and pressed on, blinded by madness, till we'd placed that ominous creature in our holy citadel. Then too Cassandra[3] opened her mouth to tell us our destined future – but the Trojans never believed her, as Apollo had ordered. And we decorated the shrines of our gods with holiday garlands, poor fools – that day was to be our last.'

250–67   As night falls the Greek fleet sails back. At a signal Sinon lets Ulysses and eight other Greeks out of the Horse – they open the gates for the rest of the troops.

'Meanwhile the sky rolled round, night rose out of the Ocean, veiling both heaven and earth and the tricks of the Greeks in darkness profound. Along the length of the walls the Trojans fell silent, their tired bodies wrapped in slumber. And now the Greek

Armada was sailing in line from Tenedos, in the moonlight's peaceful silence, heading for their familiar haunts on the shore. From the flagship a flare flamed, and Sinon, divinely protected by an unfair Fate, stealthily slid back the pine bolts of the Horse, releasing the Greeks shut inside. The Horse stood open, and from its wooden womb they gladly came out into the air, Thessander[4] and Sthenelus first, and dreadful Ulysses, sliding down the rope they had lowered; next Acamas, Thoas, Achilles' son Neoptolemus, led by Machaon, then Menelaus and Epeos, the man who'd designed the cunning contraption. They attacked our city, now buried in sleep and wine; killing the sentries, they opened the gates, admitting the rest of their mates, and joined forces according to plan.'

268–97   While the Greeks enter the city, Aeneas is asleep, like the rest of the Trojans. He dreams that Hector comes to warn him to leave Troy with the holy gods of the city. It is Aeneas' first mention of himself.

'It was the early part of the night, when the first flush of sleep, the most welcome gift of the gods, creeps over tired men. In a dream I appeared to see Hector there before me, grieving and drenched in tears, just as he was when the chariot dragged him away, dirtied with blood and dust, his feet threaded through with thongs, and swollen. Ah, what an awful sight he was, so different from the Hector who'd once come home wearing Achilles' armour, or who'd just flung our fire bombs onto their ships. His hair and beard were filthy and matted with blood: I could see all the wounds he had suffered while fighting to defend the walls of our city. I burst into tears myself, in my dream, and choked out sorrowful words.

'"Oh, saviour of Troy, the surest hope of us Trojans, what has kept you so long? Where have you come from, Hector? How good to see you at last! We're so tired of the untold casualties, all the toil and hardships that we and our city have suffered. What has so vilely disfigured your face, which used to be unmarked by trouble? Why do I see you wounded like this?"

'He took no notice of my meaningless questions, but heaving a weary sigh from the depths of his heart, said: "Aeneas, son of Venus, go, run from these flames! The enemy's taken our city.

Troy is crumbling, its highest citadels falling. You have done your duty, both to Priam and Troy – if any hands could have saved our city, mine would have done so. But now Troy entrusts to your keeping her sacred things and her gods. Take them to share your fate: find the great home for them that you are fated to build at last, after wandering far over the seas." So he spoke, and fetched the headbands,[5] the image of powerful Vesta, and the undying fire from the inmost shrine.'

> 298–317 A great din awakes Aeneas from his dream. He climbs to the roof and sees the fires raging. Realising that the Greeks have broken into the city, he runs to put on his armour.

'Meanwhile, everywhere inside the walls was plunged into a chaos of grief. The house of my father Anchises was in a remote part, set back and screened by trees, but the clamour and crash of the fighting grew horribly louder and nearer. Shaken from sleep I clambered right up to the roof-top, and stood there listening intently. It was like the sound of a fire fanned by a furious wind, raging through the cornfields, or the roar of a river in flood rampaging down from the mountains, flattening the fields and the welcome crops that the oxen have toiled for, wildly sweeping the woods away. A shepherd stands way up on a rock, and hearing the noise is bewildered and lost. So, now, the plain truth was revealed, the cunning of the Greeks plain to see. The splendid house of Deiphobus crashed to the ground, overwhelmed by the fires; next door Ucalegon's burst into flames; the reflection gleamed in the waves of the sea. I heard the shouts of the men, and the blare of trumpets; madly I snatched up my weapons without stopping to think, on fire to gather some friends to fight, to dash with them up to the citadel. Anger and fury swept me along: the glory of death in battle was all I could think of.'

> 318–60 A priest hurries up to Anchises' house, and he too tells Aeneas that the city is lost. However, Aeneas still plunges into the fighting.

'Just then Panthus appeared, Apollo's priest on the citadel. He had slipped past the Greek spears, and clutching the sacred objects, the images of our conquered gods, and dragging his tiny grandson along by the hand he ran frantically up to our doorway.

'"Panthus, where is the crucial battle? Where are we making a stand?" I cried.

'He broke in at once with a groan. "Our last hour has come, the inescapable moment of reckoning for Troy. Troy's people, Troy's city, Troy's glory, are all finished. Jupiter has savagely handed over everything to the Greeks. Our city is burning; the Greeks are its masters. Towering high over the heart of the city stands the Horse, disgorging armed soldiers, and Sinon exultantly spreads chaos with fire. Our gates are wide open, packed with the Greeks in their thousands, all that ever came here. And others are blocking the streets where they're narrow, swords drawn and ready, a sharp-pointed glittering line, waiting to kill. The sentries on guard at the gates tried to fight, but in vain, and put up a blind resistance."

'His words, and the will of the gods, carried me on, into the flames and the fighting, summoned by the madness of war, by the din, by the shouts that rose to the air. Rhipeus[6] and that formidable fighter Epytus loomed out of the moonlight and joined me: Hypanis and Dymas fell in alongside with the youngster Coroebus – he'd arrived at Troy at this time, as it happened, fired with a frantic love for Cassandra, and bringing help to us Trojans and his future father-in-law: unhappily he did not listen to his bride-to-be and her prophetic warning.

'When I saw them boldly paraded for battle, I spoke to inspire them further: "Friends, so foolishly brave! If your determination to follow me, to see everything through to the end is quite unshakeable, this is the situation. The gods who upheld our empire have gone; they've abandoned their altars and shrines; the city you want to defend is already ablaze. Let us rush into the thick of the fighting, and die! The defeated have only one hope of surviving – to give up all hope of surviving!"

'Thus was a reckless fury grafted on to their courage. Just like wolves in a dense dark fog, whose nagging hunger has sent them out prowling blindly, whose cubs wait behind in the den, their stomachs quite empty, so we ran through the enemy's missiles, towards certain death, heading straight for the heart of the city – the black night wrapped us round in a cloak of darkness.'

361–69   Aeneas interrupts his narrative with an exclamation of grief as he recalls the horrors of Troy's last night, with the dead of both sides lying in heaps.

370–401   He goes on to explain how his men are mistaken for Greeks and easily kill a band of the enemy. They disguise themselves in the Greeks' armour.

'The first Greek to cross our path was Androgeos, in command of a powerful company: mistakenly assuming we were Greek, he called out a friendly rebuke: "Hurry up, men, you're late! Why are you being so slack? The others are burning and plundering Troy: have you only just come up from the ships?" As soon as we made no convincing reply he realised that he'd fallen in with a group of Trojans. He was dumbfounded, unable to speak, and recoiled, like a man who has stepped on a snake he's not seen in a thicket of brambles, and jumps away scared as it rears up gleaming darkly, with its neck puffed out in anger. Androgeos was scared stiff at the sight of us, and tried to retreat. We charged and surrounded them, hemming them in with our swords. They were unsure of their ground and scared – we slaughtered them. Fortune was smiling on our first efforts.

'Flushed with success and fresh confidence Coroebus cried out: "Friends – this first bit of luck has shown us the way to survival – let's follow it! Let's change shields, and put on their Greek equipment. Cunning or courage, what does it matter, so long as we kill them! They'll give us the weapons!" So he put on Androgeos' plumed helmet, his shield with its splendid device, and strapped the Greek sword to his side. Rhipeus and Dymas, in fact all of the squad, cheerfully copied him, arming themselves with weapons they stripped from the dead. We advanced under borrowed protection, into the ranks of the Greeks.

'Many a battle we fought in the darkness of night, many a Greek we sent down to Hell. Some scattered in flight to their ships, and ran to the safety of the beach: some, in contemptible fear, climbed back into the enormous Horse, and made themselves snug inside it.'

402–34   They suddenly see Cassandra being dragged off as a captive. Coroebus runs to her help, and in the fighting which follows, the Trojans' disguise is uncovered.

'It is no good, alas, for anyone to put his trust in the gods if the gods don't want it! We caught sight of Priam's daughter, the maiden Cassandra, being dragged by her tangled hair from the temple and shrine of Athena, straining her burning eyes towards the heavens – but only her eyes, for her delicate hands were in chains. The sight was too much for Coroebus; madly he sprang straight at them, as if wanting to die. In close formation we charged behind him. Now, for the first time, from the roof of the temple, the spears of our fellow-Trojans rained down on us. A pitiful slaughter began, for the look of our helmets and arms made them mistake us for Greeks. Then with an angry curse at the rescue-attempt on Cassandra, the Greeks all rallied round and attacked us ... Now the party we'd deceived in the darkness, and chased in flight all over the city, put in an appearance: they were the first, alerted by our foreign tongue, to recognise the shields and swords that gave us away. At once we were overwhelmed by the weight of their numbers. The first to fall was Coroebus, slain by the hand of Peneleus at powerful Athena's altar: next died Rhipeus, the justest of all the Trojans, who always upheld what was right (though this didn't affect the gods). Hypanis and Dymas died, shot down by our comrades, and Panthus, for not all his eminent goodness nor his service as priest of Apollo could save him. I swear by the ashes of Troy and the flames that consumed my people that, throughout all their death-throes, I faced all their spears and shrank from no hazard of battle: if the Fates had meant me to die, I deserved to, for those I killed.'

434–68   Aeneas' company is scattered in the fighting, and he finds himself near Priam's palace. He sees the desperate attempt of the Trojans to defend it, and makes his way in through a secret door.

469–95   Achilles' son Pyrrhus breaks the main door down, and leads the Greeks as they storm through the palace.

'Right on the threshold of the entrance hall Pyrrhus prances triumphantly, his armour a blaze of bronze: he's just like a snake that glides into the light after a cold winter couched underground, swollen with the poisonous herbs it has fed on; now having sloughed off its skin, in gleaming bright colours, all new, it sinuously slithers its coils and lifts its head high to the sun, its forked tongue flickering. With Pyrrhus is the giant Periphas, Automedon, Achilles' charioteer and squire, and some of Achilles' men; they run up to the building, hurling fire-brands onto the roof.

'In the lead Pyrrhus himself, wielding a tough double axe, batters his way through the door, and wrenches its bronze hinge-posts from their sockets. He hacks out a hole through the solid oak planking, making a great wide opening. The palace interior, the long state-room, is revealed, the private home of Priam and earlier kings: they can see armed men on guard at the entrance. Inside is a confusion of shrieks and pitiful turmoil, and the vaulted halls ring with the wailing of women whose cries reach the golden stars. Terrified mothers flit through the echoing palace, cling to the door-posts, and kiss them. Pyrrhus attacks with his father's ferocity; neither bolts nor guards can resist him. The door succumbs to the blows of a ram, is torn from its hinges, and falls. Greek troops force their violent way in, burst through the hallway and butcher all those in their path; the whole place is packed with soldiers.'

496–505   Aeneas sees the Greeks pouring into the palace like a river in flood, killing as they go.

506–25   Then he tells how old King Priam, on seeing the Greeks in his palace, puts on his armour, and how his wife Hecuba stops him from joining the fighting.

'Perhaps you are wondering what happened to Priam. When he saw Troy's calamitous capture, the palace gates shattered and the enemy right in the heart of his home, old though he was, he slipped over his trembling shoulders the armour unused for years, strapped on his useless sword and, careless of death, turned to the thick of the fighting. In the Great Courtyard under the open sky stood the large altar, and near it an age-old bay tree, leaning over the altar and embracing the household gods in its shade. Here Hecuba and her daughters, like doves driven down to the ground by a black storm, huddled around the altar vainly seeking protection, clasping the statues of the gods. And when she saw Priam, her husband, clad in his youthful armour, she cried: "My poor husband, what fatal purpose has made you put on those things? Where are you off to? It's too late to look for help from that sort of protection, even if dear Hector himself were here. Come over here, please, with me: this altar will save us all, or else we will die together." With these words she drew the old king to her side and sat him down in the sanctuary.'

526–58 Polites, the son of the king and queen, is killed before their eyes by Pyrrhus, who then contemptuously slaughters Priam.

'Suddenly Polites, one of the sons of Priam, who had dodged the murderous sword of Pyrrhus and the rest of the enemy spears, sprints down the long colonnade, weaving his way through the empty court, wounded. An arm's length behind him, blood-crazed and poised to kill, comes Pyrrhus, at every second ready to strike with his spear. In the end, just as he reached the courtyard, right in front of his parents' eyes, Polites fell, and poured out his life in a stream of blood.

'Then Priam, though in the grip of death, did not hold back, but burst out indignantly: "You! For such a crime, for such an outrageous crime, if there's any justice in heaven to care for such things, may the gods grant you your proper reward, and give you your due deserts, for making me watch the death of my son, and fouling a father's eyes with his murder. Achilles, whom you claim as your father – you liar! – was not like that, though I was his enemy: he respected my rights and status as suppliant, gave me the bloodless remains of my Hector to bury, and sent me back home to my kingdom." As the old man spoke he hurled his pathetic spear, without any strength behind it: it clanged on the bronze shield-boss, stuck, and hung harmlessly.

'"Take a message, report all this to my father!" cried Pyrrhus, "Tell him the dismal news, how I have disgraced him. Don't forget! Now die!" Then he dragged the quavering old man, as he slipped in his son's spilt blood, right up to the altar, twined his left hand in his hair, raised the flashing blade in his right, and buried it, down to the hilt, in his side.

'Such was the end of Priam, fated, even as he died, to see his Troy burning and ruined, Troy that had once ruled proudly over so many nations and lands, mistress of Asia. The great body lay by the shore, the head hacked from the shoulders, a nameless carcass.'

'Then, for the first time, I realised the sheer horror of events. I stopped; the picture of my dear father came to me as I watched the old king, his contemporary, gasp out his life through the savage wound. I thought of Creusa, deserted, my looted home, and the fate of my little Iulus. I looked round to see what forces remained. They'd all gone, exhausted, either leaping down to the ground or throwing themselves into the fire, in despair.'

'At this very moment then, the last one still there, I caught sight of Helen lurking by the threshold of Vesta's temple and quietly hiding inside. She was revealed by the blaze of the fires, as I prowled on the roof and peered at the scenes all around. She was afraid of Trojan hatred on account of the destruction of Troy, and no less afraid of Greek vengeance and the anger of her abandoned husband. She had brought disaster to Troy and her own country alike, so the hateful woman had gone to hide at the altar. A flame of anger blazed through my heart, a fury to avenge the downfall of my country, to punish her wicked crimes.

'"Is she going to get off scot-free, to see Sparta again, and Mycenae where she was born? To return home in triumph, a queen? To see husband, home and children, with a crowd of Trojan ladies to wait on her, hand and foot? Shall she enjoy all this, with Priam dead by the sword, and Troy consumed by fire, where our shores sweated blood so often? No, never! There's no honour in punishing women, but to blot out that evil – that's a job worth doing, and I shall be praised for punishing this one – she richly deserves it. And I shall enjoy the pleasure of glutting my hatred and avenging my loved ones."'

'Such were the thoughts milling around in my maddened mind, when my gentle mother appeared to my eyes – though never before so clearly: her radiance lit up the darkness revealing that this was a goddess, with the grace and majesty known on Olympus.

'She took my hand to restrain me, letting these words fall from her rose-pink lips: "My son, why this wild resentment and ungoverned rage? What is this madness? Why have you no thought for us? Why don't you go and find out how your weary old father Anchises is, whom you left behind, and whether your wife Creusa and son Ascanius are alive? The whole Greek army is all round them, and but for my care the flames would have got them, and enemy swords spilt their blood. It is not, let me tell you, the hateful beauty of Helen of Sparta, or adulterous Paris, but the gods, the implacable gods, that have destroyed this empire and brought Troy crashing down. Look! – there's a mist that is fogging your vision and dulling your mortal eyes, that dankly wraps you in darkness: I'll sweep it away. Don't be afraid of your mother's instructions, or refuse to do what I tell you. Look at those piles of rubble, where stone has been levered from stone, and those billowing clouds of dust and smoke – it's Neptune battering the walls with his mighty trident, and demolishing the foundations; it's Neptune, digging up every stone of the city! There's Juno, brutal Juno, at the head of her troops, with her sword at her waist, guarding the gates of Troy, and calling up the reserves from the fleet. And Pallas Athena – look! – bestrides the citadel, with a halo of light around her, with the grim Gorgon's head[7] on her shield. Jupiter, too, is injecting the Greeks with courage and the strength to win, and inciting the gods to attack the Trojans. It is time to escape, my son, to put an end to your struggles. I shan't desert you; I'll see you safe home to your father's house." She spoke, and vanished into the night's dense darkness. And those fiendish shapes, those divinities hostile to Troy, were revealed.'

624–70   From the roof of the palace Aeneas watches the final ruin of Troy, like the fall of a great tree. He comes down and makes his way safely to his home. To his dismay, his father Anchises adamantly refuses to leave, preferring to die as Troy is dying. So Aeneas puts on his armour again, determined to return to the fighting.

671–91   Creusa begs Aeneas not to desert them. Then
miraculously little Iulus' hair seems to burst into flames.
Anchises recognises this as a divine omen, and prays for a sign
from heaven to confirm it.

'So I put on my sword once more, and was slipping my left arm
into the shield-strap again on the point of going outside, when, at
the doorway, Creusa clung to me, and held up the little Iulus.

'"If you are setting off to your death, then no matter what
happens, take us with you; but if your experience prompts you to
think that taking up arms is *not* hopeless, first of all fight to
defend this house! Will you leave us to someone else, Iulus, your
father and me? – I was once your wife, remember?"

'The whole house was full of her cries and groans, when
suddenly something marvellous happened, to warn us. We were
holding Iulus between us, our gaze fixed sadly upon him; from
the top of his head a thin tongue of fire flared out – the flames
harmlessly licked the soft curls and played over his forehead. In
a panic we frantically beat at the burning hair, and put out the
holy flames with some water. But my father Anchises cheerfully
raised his eyes to the stars, stretched out his hands to heaven and
prayed: "Almighty Jupiter, if ever you listen to prayers, then
listen to mine, this once: if our goodness deserves a reward, grant
us a sign, Father, to confirm this omen."'

692–706   Anchises' appeal is answered. He asks the gods for
help.

'The old man had hardly spoken, when suddenly thunder
crashed on the left, and a shooting star fell down the shadowy
sky, streaming a trail of light behind it. We saw it sail over the
roof-top and bury its brightness in the woods on Mount Ida,
marking the way we should go. A long luminous furrow was left
in its wake, and sulphurous smoke blew all round us. This was
proof enough for my father: he stood up, thanked the gods and
worshipped the holy star: "No more delay now, none! I'll follow;
wherever you lead, I'll be there. Gods of my fathers, look after
my family and grandson. Yours is the sign, and Troy is still
under your protection. My son, I consent, and no longer refuse
to go with you."'

'As he spoke the roar of the fire through the city was heard more clearly, and the tide of flames rolled nearer.'

707–44   Aeneas tells his family what they must do. They set off, and have nearly reached safety when there is a sudden panic and they take to their heels. By the time they are safely out of the city Creusa has disappeared.

'"Dear Father, quick, climb on my back! I'll carry you on my shoulders, you'll be no burden to me. No matter what happens, we'll share the same dangers together, and the same road to safety. Little Iulus shall walk at my side; let Creusa follow our footsteps, behind us. And you servants, pay attention to what I shall tell you. There's a low hill as you leave the city, and an ancient temple of Ceres[8] in mourning; near it is an old cypress tree, religiously tended for years by our ancestors. We'll all make our different ways to it, and meet there.

'"Father, you carry the sacred objects, the gods of our country. I've just come from the thick of battle with fresh blood on my hands; I mustn't touch them, till I have washed myself clean in pure running water." Then, bending my head, I covered my neck and broad shoulders with a tawny lion-skin, then stooped to pick up my burden. Iulus put his hand into mine, and trotted with quick little steps to keep up; my wife came along behind. We hurried through the shadows. Not long before, the spears thrown at me and the Greek mass attack had left me unmoved; but now every breeze unnerved me and I started at every sound, afraid for the boy beside me, afraid for the burden I carried.

'I was close to the gate now, and I thought we had got right away, when the tramping of many feet suddenly came to my ears, seemingly on top of us; peering through the shadows, my father exclaimed: "Run, my boy, run, they're close! I can see the gleam of their shields and their bronze armour glinting."

'For some reason I panicked, some unkind power stole my wits and confused me. I ran through some out-of-the-way back streets, leaving the roads I knew. Ah, poor me! Creusa, my wife, did Fate steal her from me? Did she stop? Did she lose her way? Perhaps she was tired, and sat down. Who knows? We never set eyes on her again. I never looked back to realise she was lost, never gave her a thought, until we had reached the hill and Ceres' venerable shrine. Here we all gathered at last: she was the only one missing, her loss unnoticed by her friends, her husband and son.'

745–67 Aeneas turns back into Troy to look for his wife, going first to his own home, then to her father's, only to find his own house in flames, and the palace occupied by the enemy.

'I went out of my mind, and cursed every god, every man; I'd seen nothing more bitter than this in all the ruins of our city. I committed Iulus, Anchises and our Trojan gods to the care of my friends, hiding them away in the bend of a valley. I made my way back to the city, clad again in my gleaming armour, to live every encounter again, to retrace all my steps through Troy, to face every danger once more. First I went back to the walls, and the gate we'd come out of, hard though it was to find; then I spotted my tracks and followed them in reverse, straining my eyes in the darkness. Everywhere I quaked inside, terrified even by silence. Then I returned to my home in case, just in case, she had gone there: the Greeks had burst in and occupied all of it. At this moment the hungry fire was swirled up by the wind to the roof-top, the flames shot up higher still, and the heat boiled up to the sky. I went on to her father Priam's palace, and back to the citadel. There, in the empty cloisters of Juno's sanctuary, Phoenix and grim Ulysses were on duty, guarding the booty. From all over Troy the plunder from burning temples, the gods' tables and solid gold vessels, the looted vestments, were piled up here. Around them line after line of frightened mothers and children were standing.'

768–75 Aeneas calls out Creusa's name again and again through the streets, till her ghost appears and speaks to him.

'I even dared to yell out her name through the darkness, filling the streets with my cries: sadly I called "Creusa" again and again, but it was useless. But while I was frantically running from house to house on this endless search, there appeared to my eyes an unhappy phantom, the ghost of Creusa herself, an image larger than life. I stopped, astounded: my hair stood on end, my voice stuck in my throat. Then she spoke to me, calming my fears.'

776–804   Creusa's ghost tells Aeneas that there is no need for grief. The gods have decided that they must part, but he will eventually find happiness in a country far away in the West.

'"Dearest husband, why have you given way like this to uncontrolled grief? These things have happened just as the gods decreed. You may not take Creusa with you; that's not allowed, the ruler of heaven forbids it. Long years of exile await you; a long furrow over the seas must be ploughed, till you come, in the end, to Westland, where the Tiber flows smoothly through the fine lands of its people. There you will find waiting happiness, a kingdom, a royal bride. Weep no more for your darling Creusa. I shall be spared the sight of the haughty abode of some Greek, or service to some Greek lady. I am Trojan, a daughter-in-law to Venus. No, the great mother of the gods is keeping me here. Goodbye now – and never stop loving your son and mine."

'And when she had said this she left me weeping, with so much still to say, and vanished into thin air. Three times I tried to put my arms round her neck, three times the phantom slipped through the grasp of my hands, just like a breath of wind or a fleeting dream. So at last the night came to an end. I went back to my friends.

'There I was astonished to find a great crowd, both women and warriors, newly arrived, who'd gathered to go into exile – pitiful refugees. They had come from all over the country, ready with whatever spirit and goods they could muster to follow me over the seas, to whatever country I chose. Now, over the slopes of Mount Ida the day star arose, ushering in the new day: the Greeks, in control of the city, were on guard at the gates: there was no hope of help. I turned away, picked up Anchises, and made for the mountains.'

Notes to Book II

1   **Salt meal**   The reference is to a cake, made of wheat and corn, or to loose salt and meal (= grain), used in Roman sacrifices, when it was sprinkled

over the victim's head. A woollen headband was worn by the victim, and the priest.

2   **Diomede**   During the Trojan War Ulysses and Diomede crept through the Trojan lines and stole the Palladium, a statue of Pallas Athena, because it was believed that Troy could not be captured while the Palladium was in Trojan hands.

3   **Cassandra**   A daughter of Priam. Apollo loved her, and gave her the gift of prophecy. When she resisted his advances he caused her prophecies never to be believed.

4   **Thessander**   He and the others are the nine Greek warriors shut in the Horse.

5   **headbands. . .image. . .fire**   These are the 'sacred things' mentioned a few lines earlier. Vesta was the goddess of the hearth, the personification of the home. A fire was kept burning at the hearth, and in the temple of Vesta in the city. This is a dream: Aeneas could not actually take the fire with him.

6   **Rhipeus**   Virgil likes to give a personal flavour to many incidents by using proper names, even when, as here, the characters are unimportant and do not appear elsewhere.

7   **Gorgon's head**   The three Gorgons were horrifying monsters with hideous heads with snakes for hair. Anything which met the gaze of the head was turned to stone, so representations of the heads on shields were popular.

8   **Ceres**   Goddess of corn and agriculture (hence 'cereals'); her daughter Proserpina was carried off by Hades and made queen of the Underworld. Though she returned to earth for six months of the year, Ceres constantly mourned her daughter's fate.

Book III

Aeneas continues his story in Dido's palace. After escaping from Troy, Aeneas and his companions spend the winter building a fleet, and set out on their journey round the Mediterranean in search of their promised home. This book covers six years of their wanderings.

After an unsuccessful attempt to settle in Thrace they land on Delos, the island where Apollo was born. Apollo tells them to return to 'the land which first cradled the race from which you were sprung'. So they sail on to Crete, which Anchises mistakenly believes is the place intended. But after a few months a dreadful plague forces them to leave, and a vision of their Penates, the Trojan home-gods, bids them make for Westland, which they now learn is called Italy.

They set out, but are driven by a storm up the west coast of Greece, and seek refuge in the Strophades Islands, home of the Harpies. Then the south wind takes them past Ithaca, Ulysses' home, to Actium, and thence to Buthrotum, a town in north-west Greece. This part of Greece, once ruled by Achilles, had passed to his cruel son Pyrrhus. Among the captives whom Pyrrhus had brought home from Troy as his slaves were Hector's widow, Andromache, and Helenus, another of Priam's sons. When Pyrrhus was murdered by Orestes, Helenus became king, with Andromache as his wife. They warmly welcome Aeneas and his party, who stay here for nearly a year.

However, Aeneas knows that he must sail on to Italy. He asks Helenus, who has prophetic powers, what dangers he must avoid on the way. Helenus tells him to sail down the east coast of Italy, around Sicily, then up the west coast until he reaches Cumae, where he will receive further instructions.

Aeneas obeys. On reaching Sicily he first lands near Mount Etna, where he encounters the terrifying one-eyed Cyclops, an episode recounted in the following pages. They move next to Drepanum, where Anchises dies. They set out for Italy, but are driven by a storm to Libya, and there meet Dido.

❧❧❧❧❧

In Book III the flashback continues. Aeneas comes to terms with his fate. He learns from his experiences, slowly changing from the impetuous warrior of Book II into the resourceful leader that the new community in Italy will need. It is fated that Aeneas will reach Italy, and Fate is all-powerful. But if Virgil were to let the gods whisk Aeneas immediately from Troy to Italy, men would appear mere playthings, and their existence meaningless. So Aeneas has to find his way laboriously through the real world of the Mediterranean, through various tribulations, as his future is, piece by piece, revealed to him by Apollo and his oracles.

By the time the Trojans are blown to Libya they are tired and near despair: Aeneas is tempted to stay in Carthage. But he also knows that in the end he will have to go to Italy, where a glorious future awaits his people.

Characters

Aeneas
Achaemenides, a Greek
Polyphemus, son of Poseidon. He is a Cyclops, a one-eyed giant

 588–612　In this episode the Trojans, near the end of their journey, have just sailed across the straits separating Sicily from the toe of Italy, avoiding the monstrous Scylla¹ and the whirlpool Charybdis. They have landed near Mount Etna, where they have spent the night.

'The next day dawned in the East, and sunrise had banished the dew-damp darkness from the vault of heaven, when suddenly out of the woods came a stranger, an extraordinary figure, starved skeleton-thin, dressed in rags. He stretched out his hands to us, there by the shore, imploring our help. We looked at him: appallingly filthy, his beard grown wild, his clothes pinned together with thorns: but for all that a Greek, who had once served at Troy in the army. While still some distance away, he caught sight of our Trojan weapons and clothes, and stood stock still for a second, scared by what he had seen. Then he dashed for the shore, sobbing and begging: "By the stars, by the gods above, Trojans, and the light of the air we breathe, take me with you! I don't care where you're going, just take me! I know that I sailed with the Greeks and made war on your Trojan homes, I confess it. If that's too dreadful a crime to forgive, tear me in pieces and scatter them in the wide seas to drown: if I die, I'll have died at the hands of men, no small consolation."

'He fell at our knees when he'd spoken, and clung to them, grovelling. We pressed him to tell us his name and his family, to explain the ill luck that was hounding him. After a moment, my

56

father, Anchises himself, offered the young man his right hand, a gesture which at once reassured him; and at that he cast off his fears and spoke.'

613–54 The stranger tells how he went to Troy with Ulysses, and on the way home was left behind by mistake in the cave of the Cyclops.

'"I'm from Ithaca, and came with that unfortunate man Ulysses. My name's Achaemenides. My father Adrastus was poor, so I set out for Troy – how I wish we had let things stay as they were! Here my companions left me, in the great cave of the Cyclops, forgetting me in their panic to get away from that terrible place. It's a home of blood, of blood-drenched banquets, dark inside, and vast. The Cyclops is huge, so huge that he touches the stars – dear gods, keep such a monster away from the earth! – he's unbearable to look at, impossible to talk to. He feeds on the flesh and dark blood of poor mortals. I myself saw him snatch up two of our group in that great hand of his, without moving from his couch in the cave, and crack them against a rock till the floor was spattered and swimming with blood. I saw him munching their bodies as the dark blood flowed, and their limbs were twitching, still warm, in his teeth. But he didn't get off scot-free. Ulysses wasn't a man to put up with things like that, or ever to lose his wits, no matter how fearful the crisis.

'"The Cyclops, gorged with the meal and sodden with drink, let his head droop on his chest, and sprawled out his enormous length in the cave. As he slept he vomited blood and fragments of flesh, all mingled with wine. At once we prayed to the powers above, drew lots for our places, and together surrounded him. With a sharpened stake we drilled into that enormous eye sunk deep under his savage forehead, as big as the Greek round shield or the orb of the sun. At last, with a grim joy, we avenged our slaughtered companions.

'"But run for it, quick! Run, or we're done for, break the cables away from the shore! Polyphemus is not the only one to be penning his fleecy sheep in a cave for their milk. Another hundred unspeakable Cyclopes, just as huge and hideous, live by these shores and roam over the mountain heights.

'"Three times now the crescent moon has filled with light

57

since I began dragging out my days like this in the woods, in the deserted lairs and dens of wild beasts, or watching out for those giant creatures from a rock, and trembling at the sound of their voices or footsteps. I've had a pathetic diet of berries and stony wild plums, plucked from the branches, and of the roots of plants I tore up. I've kept constant watch, yet your ships putting in to land were the first I'd seen. I vowed I'd surrender to you, whoever you were. To have escaped that unspeakable tribe, that's enough – even death, any death, at your hands would be better.'''

655–83   Aeneas and his followers catch sight of Polyphemus coming down to the shore, and make their escape.

'Achaemenides had barely finished speaking when, high on the mountains, we saw that mountainous shepherd Polyphemus, moving amongst his flock on his way to the shore he knew best, monstrous, misshapen, massive – and blind. He leant on a pine tree, stripped of its branches, to guide and support him; the fleecy sheep flock around him, his only comfort and joy in misfortune. He waded out into deep water, out to the open sea, then washed away the blood that flowed from the scooped-out eye-socket, grinding his teeth and moaning. He strode right out to mid-ocean, yet his waist was still clear of the waves.

'In alarm we hurried away, taking the Greek on board – he deserved to escape – and silently cutting the cable we swept the water behind us as we bent to the oars. Polyphemus heard, and directed his steps to the sound the oars made. He kept trying to clutch our ship in his hand, but couldn't, unable to equal the speed of the current that helped us. He let out an enormous shout – a tremor shook the whole sea-surface; Italy quaked with fright to its depths; the vaulting cavern of Etna resounded.

'The tribe of the Cyclopes, roused from the woods and mountains, hurtled down to the sea's edge, crowding the shore. We saw them, the brotherhood of Etna, standing there, each with his great grim eye, but powerless to harm us. With their heads towering up to the sky they made an awesome assembly, like soaring oak trees or cone-laden cypresses on a hill-top, a forest that's sacred to Jove or Diana. A shiver of fear made us shake out the ropes and run for it, spreading our sails to any wind that would take us away.'

684–706   The wind takes them, first south, then westward along the southern coast of Sicily.

707–18   They put in at the very westward end of Sicily, where Anchises dies. Aeneas has finished his story, and from now on Virgil again becomes the narrator.

'Then we came into harbour at Drepanum, for me a most miserable landfall. Here, alas, after so many storms at sea, I lost my father Anchises, my comfort in every trouble and misfortune . . . This was the final disaster, the turning-point of my weary travels. For on our departure, a god drove us here, to your shores.'

So Prince Aeneas, with all eyes intently upon him, recounted the course of his wanderings, the destiny which the gods had sent him. At last he came to the end of his story, was silent, and still.

Notes to Book III

1   **Scylla**   A monster which seized and devoured mariners that sailed near its cave; this overlooked the straits between Sicily and Italy, with the whirlpool of Charybdis opposite it.

Book IV

While Aeneas has been telling his story of all the events that have led up to his arrival in Carthage, Dido has been falling in love with him. All this book is about the tragedy of their love affair.

Dido tells her sister Anna that, despite her vows never to remarry, she is strongly drawn towards Aeneas. Anna advises her not to sacrifice the chance of happiness, and stresses the advantages for Carthage that would follow from marriage with Aeneas and the union of Tyrians and Trojans. A hunting expedition is interrupted by a storm: Dido and Aeneas seek shelter in a cave where, by the design of Juno and Venus, Dido lets herself be seduced.

King Iarbas, ruler of Numidia, had leased to Dido the land on which Carthage is being built, but she had rejected his offer of marriage. He now hears of the love affair and complains to Jupiter, who then reminds Aeneas of his mission to found a new city in Italy. As Aeneas prepares to leave, Dido discovers his intention; after a bitter quarrel she begs him to stay a little longer. But Aeneas sails away, and Dido kills herself, begging the gods to punish Aeneas and to make Carthage and Rome everlasting enemies.

❦❦❦❦❦

Dido is the central, tragic figure of the Book. She is gripped by a love that conquers all her pride, brushes aside all her doubts, and silences her conscience. She gives up everything for Aeneas; when he goes she has nothing left to live for.

Aeneas is, at first sight, a less than satisfactory hero. Though he never formally promises to marry Dido, knowing that his destiny insists that he must sail to Italy, he need not have stayed so long, nor let Dido imagine that he might never leave. Yet in truth his love is as strong as Dido's, so strong that, despite all he knows, he cannot resist the temptation she offers, till the direct command of Jupiter tears him away. His tragedy is that he is allowed no end for his sorrows, that he has to go on living.

Characters

Gods
Juno, patron of Carthage, goddess of marriage
Venus
Mercury, messenger of the gods

Iris, goddess of the rainbow, and messenger of Juno

Trojans
Aeneas
Ascanius (Iulus)

Carthaginians
Dido, queen of Carthage
Anna, her sister
Barce, the old nurse of Dido's dead husband Sychaeus

Places
Libya, used as a general term for north Africa, especially
    Tunisia, where Carthage is being built
Numidia, lying immediately west of Tunisia
Barce, a town in Libya (from which Hannibal's family
    came)

 1–53   Dido, falling hopelessly in love with Aeneas, confesses her
feelings to her sister Anna, but still vows never to remarry and
betray her dead husband Sychaeus. However, Anna points out all
the advantages of such a marriage.

For a long time now the queen had been painfully in love; the
beat of her heart kept the love-wound open, and a hidden fire
consumed her. The thought of the hero's great valour and the
fame of his family kept racing through her mind. His looks and
his words had pierced her heart, and stuck there, and the
anguish of love deprived her of rest and sleep.
    The dawn of the next day was moving over the earth, as the
sun's rays flung back the dew-damp curtain of darkness in the
sky, when, almost out of her mind, she spoke to her darling sister
Anna: 'Such frightening dreams! I just cannot settle to sleep!
What a man he is, this stranger we've taken into our home! How
handsome he looks, with that powerful chest and those shoulders! I believe he's the son of some god, I'm sure I'm right:
low-born men are revealed by their cowardice. Poor man, what
misfortunes he's suffered! And the wars he told of, fought to the
bitter end! If I were not unshakeably determined never again to

61

tie myself to a man in the bond of marriage, since the man I loved first betrayed me and cheated my hopes by dying, if I were not utterly sick of the idea of marriage, I might perhaps have succumbed to this one temptation.

'I'll admit, Anna, that since the death of my poor husband Sychaeus, when my brother stained our family home with his blood, this is the only man that has thrown me off balance and caused me to weaken. Once more I can feel the stirring of passion. But I pray that the earth may gape wide open to take me, that the Almighty Father may blast me down to the pale ghosts and pitch black of the Underworld, before I outrage my conscience and dishonour my vows to the man who first made me his wife. When he died he took down with him my right to love: let him keep it, down in his tomb, for ever.' She spoke, then choked on a flood of tears.

Anna replied: 'Dear sister, you are more to me than the light of day. Why should you waste all your youth in sorrow and loneliness, without ever knowing the joy of children, or the comfort of love? Do you think that the ashes of the dead, or ghosts in a tomb, will care? Perhaps: I know that no suitors in Libya, or before that in Tyre, ever found a way to your wounded heart. You rejected Iarbas, and not a few other powerful African kings. But now there's a love that attracts you, why fight it?

'Remember whose land you have settled in: you're encircled by Gaetulian cities – and they're hard to beat in war – and by Numidian horsemen who never let anyone tame them. Off shore there are unfriendly sand-banks – and then there's the waterless desert and the wide, mad, sway of the city of Barce. I don't need to mention the prospects of war with Tyre, and the threats of your brother. It's my belief that the Trojans were blown here through divine providence and the blessing of Juno. What a fine city and empire you'll see growing here, dear sister, with a husband like that! And think what glory Carthage will rise to with Trojan arms on our side! Just ask the gods for their favour, make the right offering, then ply Aeneas with rich hospitality, find excuse after excuse for delay while storms and rainy Orion[1] are raging at sea, while his ships are still shattered and the weather prevents him sailing.'

54–89 Dido is persuaded, and arranges a sacrifice. She is burning with passion, and wounded, like a deer hunted by some shepherd. She spends all her time with Aeneas, and while she does so all the work of building Carthage comes to a halt.

With these words Anna fans the spark of love in her sister's heart to a flame, replaces hesitation with hope, and loosens the shackles of conscience. First they go to the shrines, searching for peace of mind at their altars. They sacrifice ritually selected ewes to Ceres,[2] who gave men laws, to Apollo and the venerable Wine-God, but to Juno above all others, for her concern for the sanctity of marriage. Dido, in all her loveliness, herself takes the chalice and pours the libation between the horns of a milk-white cow; and in front of the statues of the gods, she walks to their altars glistening with fat from the victims. She makes a fresh start each day with an offering; when the victims are opened up she hangs over them, to find guidance from the still-throbbing entrails.[3] But soothsayers, sadly, don't know everything. Temples and prayers are no help to a woman who is madly in love. A flame is still eating away at her gentle heart, and the love-wound secretly lives on in her breast. Poor Dido is afire with love, and roams all over the city in a frenzy. She's like a deer, caught unaware by a long arrow-shot in some Cretan wood which a shepherd has fired in a ruthless volley, leaving the flying steel in her. He does not know it, but the deer reels away through the woods and glades of Mount Dicte, with the deadly shaft fixed fast in her side.

Now Dido parades Aeneas with her through the length and breadth of the city, displaying the power of Phoenicia and Carthage all ready for him. She begins to speak, then breaks off with the words half-spoken. As the day slips away she wants the banquet repeated, wildly begging to hear once more the terrible story of Troy, and hangs on his lips as he tells it again.

Then, when they part, and the moon in its turn dims its light, and the stars as they set bid her sleep, she's alone and the house is empty. Sadly she lies on the couch he has sat on, sees him and hears him still, though he's gone. Sometimes, fascinated by Ascanius' likeness to his father, she imagines him still on her lap, as if to deceive the love she won't even admit to herself.

Meanwhile all work on the half-built towers comes to a standstill; no one bothers with tools, or with building defences and harbours to ward off the threats of war. Everything grinds to a halt, the great lowering walls, the buildings rearing up to the sky.

90–104 The scene changes to Olympus, home of the gods. Juno suggests a truce: let Aeneas marry Dido and have Carthage as her dowry.

As soon as Jupiter's dear wife, the daughter of Saturn, was quite sure that Dido was trapped, and ready to give up her good name for her passion, she made an approach to Venus.

'A marvellous feat, to be sure, a rich victory for you and your boy! Your great powers will win lasting acclaim if two gods have managed to beat one woman – by a trick! I know perfectly well that you fear my city, and regard the welcoming homes of high Carthage with deep suspicion. But where will our rivalry end, how far will it go? Wouldn't it be better to arrange a marriage between them, then settle for peace everlasting? You've got what you wanted; Dido is burning with love, mad passion fills the very core of her being! So let's govern a united people between us, with equal authority: let her marry her Phrygian husband and become his slave, and surrender her Tyrian subjects to you, for her dowry.'

105–28 Venus says that she would agree at once if Jupiter approved. Juno is sure of his consent, and suggests a scheme to bring about the marriage, to which Venus agrees.

Venus was aware that Juno lied, that she wanted to divert to Libya the empire that was meant to be Rome's, so she answered like this: 'Who would be crazy enough to reject such terms, and to choose war with you instead? May fortune favour the scheme you propose. But Fate makes me full of misgivings, whether Jupiter wants there to be one city for Tyrians and Trojan exiles, and approves of this fusion of peoples and a treaty between them. You're his wife; you're entitled to tamper with his feelings. Go on; I'll be right behind you.'

Juno's regal reply was as follows: 'Leave that task with me. Now, as to the method of achieving the matter in hand, listen and I'll briefly explain. Aeneas and poor love-sick Dido intend to go hunting tomorrow in the forests as soon as the sun has risen and unveiled the world with its rays. While the beaters are bustling about and ringing the woods with their nets, I'll pour down upon them a dark rain-storm spattered with hail, and rattle the heavens with thunder. Their companions will scatter for shelter, blotted out by a darkness of night, but Dido and the Trojan leader will arrive at the same cave together. I shall be there and, provided you give me your blessing, shall join them in the firm bonds of marriage, and declare her his true wife. That shall be their wedding.'

Venus nodded assent to her scheme, and smiled at the cunning behind it.

129–59   The hunting party assembles at dawn. In the
mountains they find plenty of game – Ascanius especially
distinguishes himself.

Meanwhile dawn arose from the Ocean. As the light grew stronger, the pride of Carthage poured from the gate, carrying nets of fine mesh, snares and broad-bladed hunting spears: out poured the African horsemen, and a pack of keen-scented hounds. The queen was taking her time in her room, while the leading Carthaginians waited at the gate of the palace; and there stood her steed, resplendent in purple and gold, high-spirited, champing its foam-flecked bit. At last came the queen, with a crowd of courtiers to attend her, and a Sidonian cloak with its bright-coloured fringe flung over her shoulders. Her quiver was fashioned from gold: gold was the clasp in her hair, and golden the brooch that fastened her deep scarlet dress. There too came her Trojan friends, and gleeful Iulus. Then Aeneas, by far the most handsome, took his place at her side, joining his forces with hers.

He was like Apollo when, leaving his winter home by his river in Asia, he visits his birthplace, Delos, to start up the Spring Dances again, and his worshippers noisily flock round his altar. Apollo himself strides over the highest slopes on the island, his long flowing hair confined in a soft wreath of bay leaves and a circlet of gold, with his arrows rattling on his shoulder. Aeneas' movements were as active as his, and the radiance on his princely face was as bright.

When they'd arrived at the mountains and pathless woods, they spotted wild goats, dislodged from the crags above them, dropping down from the peak. In another direction stags went racing across open ground, and the dust clouds followed the herds as they fled from the mountains. But down in the valley, young Ascanius, making the most of his spirited horse, galloped past group after group, praying that instead of such easy sport as the deer he might meet a wild foaming boar, or a bronze-coloured lion padding down from the heights.

160–72 A storm breaks – everyone runs for shelter, and Dido and Aeneas reach the same cave together. The forces of nature witness their union, and it is from this that their tragedy begins.

At this point a rumble and grumble of thunder began, followed by rain and hail; Tyrians and Trojans, hunters and courtiers together, and the grandson of Venus, scattered and scampered for shelter, as torrents poured down the mountain. Dido and Aeneas arrived at the same cave. Primeval earth, and Juno, goddess of marriage, gave the sign. Lightning flashes and air witnessed their union; high up above them nymphs howled. That day was the beginning of sorrow, the beginning and cause of death. No longer was Dido concerned with appearances or her own reputation, no longer did she think of keeping her love affair quiet. She called it a marriage, masking her sin with a word.

173–97 Rumour runs through Libya, mingling truth and lies, alleging that Dido and Aeneas are living together. Iarbas, one of Dido's former suitors, hears the news.

At once Rumour raced through the great cities of Libya, Rumour the swiftest of all evil things, Rumour that feeds on movement, gathering strength as she goes. Small and nervous at first, she soon sprouts up into the air, and while still treading the earth carries her head cloud-high. She was the first of the children of Earth . . . swift on her feet and wings, a huge terrifying monster. Incredible as it may sound, every feather on her body has a snooping eye beneath it, and a whispering mouth and tongue, and an ear ready to eavesdrop. At night she flies through the dark, wings whirring, midway between earth and sky, never closing her eyes in sweet sleep. By day, like a look-out, she perches on the roof of a house or high tower, intimidating great cities, for she's as ready to spread warped lies as to blurt out the truth.

This time she gleefully filled the ears of the people with all sorts of scandal, a mixture of lies and truth: she told of the arrival of Aeneas, prince of the Trojan blood, and how Dido, their beautiful queen, thought fit to call him her husband: how they were comfortably spending the long winter months in debauchery, forgetting their kingdoms, ensnared by their shameful passions. These were the tales that the loathsome goddess dripped into men's mouths, throughout the land. Then she sped straight to the king Iarbas, setting his heart on fire with her words, and heaped up his anger.

198–218 Iarbas, on hearing the news, indignantly reproaches Jupiter as a weakling for allowing him to be scorned by a foreign woman and her effeminate lover.

Iarbas was Jupiter's son from an affair with an African nymph. Throughout his extensive kingdom he had built a hundred great temples in honour of his father, and made three hundred altars holy with undying flames, to keep watch for the gods for ever; the earth was enriched with the blood of victims, doorways were wreathed in a rainbow of flowers. He was out of his mind, and seared by these bitter rumours: they say that in front of the altar, in the majestic presence of the gods, he raised his hands humbly in prayer: 'Almighty Jupiter, to whom now even the Moors, when they dine from their painted couches, pour out an offering of wine, do you see what has happened? Father, are we foolish to quake at the blast of your thunderbolts? Are your terrifying flashes of lightning fired from the clouds without aim? Are the rumblings they cause quite harmless? The woman who strayed to my land and built that puny city of hers for a price – I gave her a piece of the shore to plough, on a lease – has rejected my offer of marriage, and welcomed Aeneas into her palace as lord and master. And now that soft creature, with his effeminate gang, with a head-scarf over his perfumed hair and tied under his chin, is making the most of his prize, while we keep on bringing gifts to your temples, as if you were really there, and foster your fame, all for nothing.'

219–37 Jupiter responds at once by sending Mercury down to Aeneas to remind him of his duty to find a new home for Troy.

Mercury must tell him that he has no right, even if he has lost his own ambition, to ruin Ascanius' future.

As Iarbas embraced the altar and argued his case, all-powerful Jupiter heard him and turned his gaze on Carthage and on those lovers, now so careless of public opinion. So then he addressed Mercury and gave him his instructions: 'Come, my son, off you go! Summon the winds, and wing your way down. Speak to the Trojan prince, who's still waiting in Tyrian Carthage, never thinking of the cities which the Fates have marked down as his: use the speed of the winds to take him my message. It wasn't a man like this that his beautiful mother promised us; it wasn't for this that she rescued him twice from the spears of the Greeks. This would be the man, she said, to be ruler of Italy, a land seething with wars, with the chance of supreme command: this would be the man to pass on the noble blood-line of Troy, and to make the whole world obedient to law. If the honour of such an achievement no longer fires his ambition, if he no longer makes any responsible effort for the sake of his own reputation, does Ascanius' father grudge his own son the city of Rome? What is he up to? What does he hope to gain by delaying with a hostile nation, forgetting the Italian people and the lands of Lavinium? He must sail! That's the long and the short of it. Let that be my message.'

238–78   Mercury flies straight to Carthage, stopping only at the peak of Mount Atlas. Finding Aeneas in charge of the building of the new city, he delivers Jupiter's message, and vanishes.

When he had spoken, Mercury set about obeying his great father's commands. First he bound on his feet the golden sandals which carry him aloft on their wings over land and sea alike on a swirling current of air. Then he picked up his wand – with it he summons pale spirits from the Underworld or sends others down to that sad place; with it he gives sleep or withholds it, and opens men's eyes at death to allow them to see where they're going. Now he used it to marshall the winds, and swam through the storm clouds. Then on his flight he glimpsed the peak and steep sides of Atlas, that bleak mountain that holds up the sky on its summit ... Here he first came to rest, gliding in on beautifully balanced wings: from here, with all the strength of his body, he dived down to the sea like a bird which flies low and close to the water, by the shores and the rocks, for fish.

As soon as he set his winged feet on the huts, he caught sight of Aeneas superintending the work on the new houses and battlements. His sword was studded with glittering jasper, the cloak that hung from his shoulders was glowing in Tyrian purple, interwoven with fine threads of gold. In spite of her wealth, Dido had made it herself, as a personal gift. Mercury went straight for him.

'Are you now playing the attentive husband, laying foundations for Carthage to rise on, building a beautiful city? You've forgotten your own kingdom, and your future. The king of the gods himself, who has absolute power over heaven and earth, sent me down through the air from sunny Olympus, with this express message for you: "What are you up to? What do you hope to gain by idly wasting your time on Libyan soil? If the glory of great achievements no longer stirs you, have some thought for the growing Ascanius and his hopes of claiming his rightful inheritance, a kingdom in Italy on Roman soil."' With these words, even while he was speaking, he faded from human sight, and vanished far from their eyes into thin air.

279–95   Aeneas is appalled by this warning. Anxious to obey, he wonders how to tell Dido. Eventually he orders his men to make secret preparations to depart, hoping to find some suitable opportunity for breaking the news to the queen.

Aeneas was struck dumb by this vision, and witless: his hair stood on end in horror; his voice stuck fast in his throat. He was afire to get away quickly, to leave this land behind him, much as he loved it, shaken by such an imperious warning from heaven. What on earth could he do? How dare he approach the queen now, when she was madly in love? What words could he find to begin? His thoughts darted this way and that, grasping at any idea, considering all possibilities. And then he made up his mind; this was the plan that seemed best. He summoned Mnestheus, Sergestus and brave Serestus: he told them quietly to fit out the fleet, to collect the crews on the shore, to get the tackle all ready, and to disguise the reason for this change of plan. In the mean time, since his darling Dido knew nothing, and did not suspect that their great love was falling apart, he would puzzle out how to approach her, the kindest moment to speak, the best way to act. They cheerfully did as he told them and hurried to obey his commands.

296–330   But a rumour reaches Dido. She rushes through the city, violently accuses Aeneas of trying to deceive her, and begs him to change his mind.

But who could deceive a woman in love? The queen, apprehensive even when all was well, and instinctively sensing deception, was the first to hear what was going to happen. The self-same mischievous Rumour that spoke to Iarbas told her, so madly in love, that the fleet was being made ready to sail. Completely out of control, and furious, she stormed all over the city, like a woman possessed.

At last she let fly at Aeneas before he could utter a word: 'Cheat! Did you think you could hide such a criminal act, and slip away from my land unheard? Doesn't our love keep you here, or the vows you once swore, or even the thought of the miserable death I shall suffer? All this hard work at your ships in winter, all this hurry to sail when the north winds are at their worst – how cruel! Supposing that Troy were still as it used to be, that you were sailing back to your old haunts in your own home country, would you still be braving the storm on a voyage to Troy? Is it *me* that you're running away from?

'By these tears of mine, by the hand you gave me – in my sorrow I've nothing else left – by our wedding, the marriage we've hardly begun, if ever I've helped you or pleased you even a little, pity my failing home, I beg you: if there's any place left for prayers, please change your mind! Thanks to you the Libyans, the Nomad chieftains, hate me, the Tyrians resent me, too; thanks to you I sacrificed my virtue, and the good name I once had, the one hope I had of undying fame. If you go, dear guest, what have I left to live for? (What else can I call you but "guest" – you're no husband now!) What am I waiting for? For my brother Pygmalion to smash down my city? For Iarbas to take me and marry me? Ah, if only, before you left, I could have held your child in my arms, nothing more; if only a baby Aeneas were playing in the palace to remind me of you by his looks – then at least I would not be feeling so utterly trapped and deserted.'

331–61   Aeneas hides his own sorrow, replying that it is his duty to leave.

She stopped speaking. And he, remembering Jupiter's words, kept his gaze steady, and with a great struggle repressed his feelings. In the end he offered a brief reply: 'I shall never deny the countless kindnesses which you can rightly claim you have done me; I shall always remember Dido with pleasure, as long as I remember myself and there's breath in my body. Let me say a few words about us. I never intended to slink away stealthily, don't think I did. I never offered you marriage, or went through a marriage ceremony. If the Fates allowed me to live my life as I wished and to settle my own affairs, my first thoughts would be for Troy and the precious remains of my people: a palace would stand there again, and I would have rebuilt the city, for its defeated people. But Italy, great Italy, is the land I must make for, commanded to do so by Apollo and his Lycian oracles; there is my heart and homeland now.

'You are Phoenician: if you are kept here by Carthage and the sight of your Libyan city, how can you grudge us Trojans the chance to settle in Italy? We too have the right to look for a kingdom abroad. Whenever the night comes, covering the earth in dew-damp darkness, whenever the bright stars rise, in my dreams the troubled ghost of my father Anchises alarms me with a frightful warning: so too does the thought of Ascanius, and the wrong that I'm doing my son, whom I'm cheating of his kingdom in Westland, and the country he's destined to rule. Just now, too, the messenger of the gods was despatched through the racing breezes by Jupiter himself – I swear it, on your life and mine – to bring me his orders. With my own eyes, in broad daylight, I saw the god coming inside these walls, and with my own ears I took in his every word. Your reproaches torment us both – please stop. Though it's not what I'd choose myself, I *am* going to Italy.'

All the time he was speaking Dido kept her head turned to one side, but watched him, letting her eyes roam all over him, without uttering a sound. Then furiously she spoke her mind.

'You're not the son of a goddess, you treacherous lout, or of fine old Trojan stock! The harsh rocks of the Caucasus gave you birth, Caspian tigers their milk! Why should I hide my feelings? – there cannot be worse to come! Did he sigh when I wept? Did he spare me a glance? Did he soften, show any sorrow, or pity me when I loved him? I hardly know what to put first. At the moment great Juno and almighty Jove himself have lost all sense of justice. Nowhere can trust be trusted. I welcomed him when he was shipwrecked and destitute; like a mad fool I gave him a share in my kingdom. I found him his missing fleet, and rescued his friends from death (I'm on fire, and shaking with frenzy!). Now, so he says, it's Apollo, god of prophecy, now the Lycian oracles, now the messenger of the gods as well, despatched by Jupiter himself that brings through the air the command he dreads. As if the gods above would be bothered with this, or let this disturb their tranquillity!

'I won't detain you, or question your word. Go – let the winds take you to Italy, find your kingdom over the seas! My only hope is that you'll end up on some mid-ocean rock – there must be *something* the powers of goodness can do – and drain the cup of my vengeance, calling out "Dido" again and again. Though far away, I'll pursue you with black-smoke flames, and when the chill of death has set my soul free from my body, my spirit will haunt you, wherever you go. You'll pay for your cruelty then! I shall hear, and the news of your paying will come down to the Underworld.'

With these words she broke off, with her answer unfinished; in her misery she fled indoors, swept away out of sight, leaving him alarmed and uncertain, yet ready with a hundred answers. Her servants caught her up as she fainted, carried her limp form to her cool white room, and carefully laid her down.

But Aeneas, aware of his duty, though he longed to ease Dido's sorrow with comforting words, and to put an end to her troubles, though he sighed and sighed, though his heart, for all his resolve, was shaken by the depth of his love, still obeyed the commands of the gods and went back to the fleet. Then the Trojans really went to work, dragging the tall ships down along the length of the beach. They launched the newly tarred hulls, brought leafy branches to make oars, and unfinished timbers from the woods, in their hurry to be gone.

From every part of the city you could see them moving out, and hurrying along. They were like an army of ants, which, mindful of winter, rob a great heap of corn and store it in their home: the black column tramps over fields, carting the loot along narrow paths through the blades of grass; some of them push with their shoulders, heaving the immense grains along; others are marshalling the line, and rounding up stragglers; the whole path is a bustle of activity.

What were your feelings then, Dido, as you gazed at all this? How deep were your sighs when you looked out from the top of the citadel at the shore, seething with men end to end, and saw the whole reach of the sea a mass of confusion and noise? How ruthless love is in driving men's hearts to extremes! So Dido was driven once more to see what entreaties and tears might achieve, and humbly to make her proud spirit bow down to her love, in case she left something untried, and went to a needless death.

416–36   Dido points out to Anna the Trojans getting ready to depart, and asks her to do one thing for her, to ask Aeneas to wait for fair weather, so that with time she may learn to bear her sorrow.

'Anna, you see the bustle down there, on every part of the beach? There's not a Trojan left in the city; already the sails are up and inviting the wind, and the sailors have garlands of flowers on their ships in their joy at departing. This dreadful misery of mine – I was able to foresee it once, I shall be able to endure it now. But Anna dear, just do this one thing for your poor sister. Only to you would that treacherous creature listen, or confide even his most secret feelings. You alone know the soft approach and the tactful moment to speak to him. So Anna, please go down and make humble appeal to our arrogant enemy. *I* never conspired with the Greeks to destroy the Trojan people; *I* never sent a fleet against Troy; *I* have not disturbed the ashes or soul of his father Anchises – so why does he stubbornly refuse to let my words move him? Why is he rushing away? Let him grant me, his miserable lover, this final favour, to wait for following winds and an easier voyage. I'm not asking for the honourable state of marriage – he has betrayed it! Nor do I ask him to do without lovely Latium, and to give up his kingdom. All I want is just time, some quiet and rest from the tempests of love, till I learn from misfortune how to bear with the pain of defeat. This is the last favour I have to beg – so pity your unhappy sister; and after he's granted it, I'll repay him ten times over at the time of my death.'

437–73   But Anna's words have no effect on Aeneas, so Dido, terrified of the future, makes up her mind to die: terrible omens strengthen her determination.

These were Dido's prayers, and this was the tearful tale that her unhappy sister kept taking to him. But Aeneas was unmoved by tears, inflexible, deaf to all words. The Fates barred the way, the gods blocked the kind ears of the man.

Sometimes wintry storms in the Alps, gusting from every direction, struggle to root up a sturdy oak tree whose years give it strength: the branches creak, the tree-trunk shakes as the topmost leaves rain to the ground, but the tree clings fast to the rock, as its roots go deep down towards Hell as far as its head reaches up to the sky. In just the same way is Aeneas battered by insistent pleas from every side, and his great heart feels the full force of the suffering; but his purpose stays firm, and the tears roll down in vain.

Then was poor Dido truly terrified by what was in store for her; tired of her life on earth, she prayed for death. And as if to make her more willing to act and to give up her life, when placing her offerings on the altar flaming with incense, she saw a horrible thing; the holy water turned black, and the wine she was pouring changed obscenely into blood. She told no one of what she had seen, not even her sister. Worse was to come: there was in the palace a marble shrine to her first husband's memory, which she tended with marvellous care, decorating it with hangings of snow-white wool and festive greenery. When the darkness of night enveloped the world, she thought she heard words coming from this shrine, the voice of her husband calling her; and a solitary screech-owl on the roof-top hooted in sepulchral lament, and its repeated call lengthened into a long, last, wail. Furthermore, numerous predictions of ancient prophets made her shudder with their dreadful warnings. In dreams Aeneas furiously pursues her to madness; or else she is forever being abandoned, eternally treading an endless road in a lonely desolate land in search of her Tyrians . . .

474–521 Dido has decided how she is to die. To deceive her sister she pretends that a sorceress has told her how to win back Aeneas, or else how to cure herself of her love for him. She needs, she says, a funeral pyre. Anna unsuspectingly helps her make it.

So when she was overcome by her grief she conceived a mad idea, and determined to die. All by herself in secret she worked out the time and the method; masking her scheme with a calm and hopeful expression, she addressed her unhappy sister: 'Dear Anna! Good news at last! Wish me joy of it! I have found a way to get back his love, or to free me of mine. Next to the edge of Ocean where the sun sets, is the country of Ethiopia. It's there that great Atlas holds on his shoulders the star-studded sky as it wheels around. I was told of a sorceress from there, a Numidian; she was wardress of the temple of the Daughters of Evening;[5] she used to give the dragon its food – sprinkling it with oozing honey and poppy seeds to lull it to sleep (it guarded the tree from whose branches hung the golden apples). She boasts that she can with her spells free anyone's heart from the chains of love, if she wishes, or impose love-pangs on others; she'll bring river waters to a stop, turn stars back in their course, or conjure up spirits in the night – you'd see the earth rumble beneath your feet, and ash trees troop down the mountains.

'The gods and you, dear Anna, my beloved sister, must see how reluctant I am to resort to magic. But, please, secretly build a tall pyre for me in the inner court of the palace: put on it the sword which the hero left hanging up in the bedroom (he forgot his duty then!) and every last thing that he wore, as well as the marriage bed which has been the cause of my downfall. I want to destroy everything that calls that villainous man to mind, and the sorceress, too, bids me do it.'

Then she fell silent, and her face grew pale. But Anna still had not guessed that her sister was using this strange ceremonial as a cover for suicide, she had no idea of the extent of her sister's madness, and didn't fear anything worse than had happened on the death of Sychaeus. So she did what Dido had asked.

When, in the very heart of the palace, the pyre had been built up high with pine-wood and logs of oak, the queen hung the place with garlands and a funeral wreath up above. On top she put his clothes, the sword he had left, and on the bed an effigy of him: *she* knew what was going to happen. Altars were set up around it. The sorceress, with hair let loose, thundered a prayer to three hundred gods – to Erebus,[6] Chaos and Hecate three-in-one, the three-faced virgin Diana. She sprinkled water – it came from the springs of Hell, so she said – and herbs from her store, which she'd culled by moonlight with a sickle of bronze, oozing a black poisonous sap; and from her store she took a love-charm, torn from the brow of a foal at the moment of birth before its mother could get it. Dido herself at the altar made the reverent offering of salt and ground corn: she'd left one foot bare, and undone the belt of her dress. Then, so near now to death, she called on the gods and the stars that share the secrets of destiny to observe what she did, and prayed to the power, whatever it is, that, caring and just, looks after the victims of one-sided love.

522–52 When night comes Dido cannot sleep. Then, irrationally, she turns on her sister, and blames Anna for causing all her suffering.

Now it was night, and weary bodies all over the world were enjoying the comfort of sleep; forests and rough seas had grown quiet as the stars wheeled round half-way towards their setting. Every field was silent; the cattle, the bright-coloured birds by the broad clear lakes, or in the tangled woods of the countryside, all still and asleep in the silence of night, were soothing away their cares, and hearts forgot pain.

But not so the poor queen of Carthage, her distress was too great; she could never relax in sleep or let night steal over her eyes or heart. Her anguish redoubled; waves of love flooded fiercely back, seething in a great tide of passion. This was the insistent pattern, the vicious circle of her thoughts: 'What am I doing? Must I make a fool of myself, and go crawling back to my former suitors and, though time after time I've rejected their offers, beg one of the African kings to marry me? Shall I follow the Trojan fleet, and obey their final "Come with us!"? Will they still remember how grateful they were for my kindness, for the help that I gave them? Even supposing I wanted to, who would accept me and allow me aboard their arrogant ships? They hate me! I'm ruined, alas: surely I should know by now what a treacherous people they are! And if I do go – do I run off by myself to become a "friend" of rollicking sailors? Or shall I sail off with the Tyrian guard all around me? I was only just able to tear them away from Tyre: can I force them to sea again, to sail where the winds may take them?

'No! I must die – I deserve to – and put an end to my pain with this sword. Anna, you started it all, you gave in to my tears, then loaded me up with enough sorrow to drive me mad and put me at the enemy's mercy. You wouldn't let me stay innocently unmarried like some creature of the wild, and so avoid this miserable sort of affair. I have not kept faith with the vows I made to my dear dead husband Sychaeus.'

553–83   Meanwhile Aeneas is asleep, intending to sail at dawn.
In a dream Mercury reappears to warn him that Dido's anger
means danger, and that he must set off at once.

Such were the angry complaints that kept bursting out in her heart. Aeneas, now that he had decided to leave, was fast asleep high up in the stern of his ship: everything had been made ready to sail. There came to him in a dream the vision of the god, returning with the same appearance as before, and with much the same warning – exactly like Mercury, in voice, complexion, blond hair, a fine and youthful physique.

'Son of a goddess, how can you sleep at a time like this? Are you crazy, to be so blind to the dangers that will soon be upon you? Can you not hear the favourable west wind blowing? That woman is set upon death, a prey to the varying tide of passions – she's hatching some plot, some dreadful crime in her heart. Why don't you run for it, hurry away while hurry you can? Soon, if dawn finds you lingering still in this land, you will see the ocean in a turmoil of moving timbers, firebrands aimed fiercely at you, the beach all ablaze. Off with you! No more delay! Women are always inconstant, changeable things.' So he spoke and vanished into the gloom of night.

Then Aeneas, startled by this sudden apparition, shook himself awake and shouted his crew on deck: 'Jump to it, men! To your places, stand by the oars! Up sail, hoist away! Once more a god – from heaven above, look, a god – is goading us on to cut the strands of the cables and run for it. And it's the second time! We follow you, holy of gods, whoever you are, and again we obey your commands, exultantly. Be with us, grant us your kindly aid, bring on the right stars to guide us.' He spoke, snatched his sword from its scabbard, and with the flashing blade slashed at the stern-ropes. The same urgent haste gripped them all; they hurried and scurried, abandoned the shore, covered the water with ships, heaving and straining and churning the deep blue sea into foam.

584–629   As dawn breaks, Dido sees the Trojans sailing away.
She begs the gods to send Aeneas every form of cruel misfortune
both on his voyage and on reaching land. She prays that Carthage
and Rome may be everlasting enemies. (Her very last words must
have brought the memory of Hannibal into every Roman mind.)

The new dawn, leaving her husband's golden bed, was shedding fresh light on the earth. From her roof-top the queen saw the sky turn pale and the fleet moving ahead, all sails in line; saw that the shore and harbour were empty, the crews all gone. Three times and again she beat her lovely breast with her hand, and tore the fair hair from her head.

'By god, will that foreigner go, and succeed in making a joke of my royal power? Will my people not take up arms, and from all over Carthage pursue him? Won't some of them pull the ships out of dock? Get a move on, quick, fetch your weapons and fire, heave at the oars! What am I saying? Where am I? What madness is turning my mind? Poor Dido, is your wickedness only now coming home to you? You should have thought of that at the time when you offered him a share of your throne. So much for his word of honour! And they say that he carries the statues of his home-gods with him, and took his doddering old father on his back! I could have torn up his body and scattered the sea with its pieces – why didn't I? I should have slaughtered his friends with the sword, Ascanius too, and served him up for his father to feast on! It would have been a dangerous, uncertain battle – what of it? I was going to die anyway, so I had no one to fear. I should have set fire to his camp, burnt all his ships, wiped out father and son, and his people, then thrown myself on the flames.

'I call on the Sun, whose light is turned on everything that men do on earth; and Juno, agent and witness of all my distress; and Hecate, greeted with howls in the night wherever three roads meet; and the avenging Furies of Hell – any god who heeds my voice as I die: hear me, hear my prayers! Bring your powers to bear on my sorrows, give them their due reward. If this foul creature must find journey's end on land, if that is ordained by Jupiter's will and cannot be altered, then let him be hounded in war by the swords of a valiant people, exiled far from his home, torn from the arms of Iulus and driven to plead for help. Let him watch his friends die unworthy deaths. And when at last he surrenders to the terms of an unfair peace, may he never enjoy his rule, or a long life of happiness. Let him die before death is due, unburied, on an open shore. This is my prayer: as I pour out these final words, I pour out my life-blood too.

'You now, my Tyrian people – never stop hating his children, and his children's children to come! Grant this last gift in remembrance of me. Let there be no love, no treaty between our peoples. Let someone arise from my bones to avenge me, to harry these Trojan settlers with fire and steel, today, tomorrow, whenever the strength is granted. Shore against shore, sea against sea, sword against sword, this is my curse upon them; let them fight each other to the last generation!'

630–50 Dido moves towards her final act. She sends Barce to tell Anna to bring everything else needed to complete her 'magic sacrifice'.

With this curse she started turning over in her mind every possibility, to find the swiftest end to the life she now hated. She spoke briefly to Barce, Sychaeus' old nurse, for her own was but dust and ashes buried in Tyre.

'Dear nurse, would you please bring my sister here? Tell her to be quick and sprinkle herself with river-water, and to bring with her the cattle I was told to sacrifice in atonement. That's how she must come, and you must put on your sacred headband. I have prepared and ceremonially started these rites to the god of the Underworld – and now I intend to conclude them, and so put an end to my troubles by committing to flames the pyre of that Trojan creature.'

When she had spoken the nurse bustled off like the fussy old woman she was. But Dido, trembling like some wild animal at her monstrous schemes, her eyes bloodshot and rolling, her cheeks quivering, stained by bright patches, but pale, for death was now near, burst into the inner courtyard, climbed in her frenzy to the top of the pyre and drew the sword, the Trojan sword she had asked as a gift, though not for this purpose! But then, on catching sight of his clothes, and their familiar bed, she paused a moment, for tears and remembrance, then lay down on the bed, and spoke for the very last time.

651–71 Dido recalls the great achievements of her life, then curses Aeneas for betraying her, and stabs herself. A cry of despair from her attendants spreads through the palace.

'These mementoes of him – they gave me such pleasure while the Fates and the gods allowed – let them take this life of mine, and release me from all my cares. I have lived a full life; now I've come to the end of the span which fortune has given me; now my ghost will go in glory to the world below. The city I have built is famous; I have seen its walls completed; I have avenged my husband, and punished my hateful brother. I would have been happy – too happy, perhaps – if only those Trojan ships had never put in to our land!'

She spoke, and buried her face in the bed; then again: 'No one will avenge my death – but still, let me die. This, this is the way I'm determined to die. Let the cruel Trojan's eyes, from far out at sea, gaze long on the flames from the pyre, and take with him the bad-luck omen of my death.'

As she spoke her attendants saw her suddenly fall on the sword, saw it foaming with blood, and blood pouring over her hands. A shriek shrilled up to the roof: the city was stunned as

Rumour raved through it. Sad cries, groans and the wailing of women rang through the palace, the heavens resounded with great lamentation. It was just as if Carthage, or ancient Tyre, were being totally sacked by invading enemy troops, and flames were furiously rolling high over the homes of men and of gods.

672–92   Anna hears the commotion and realises the cause. As she hurries to Dido she reproaches her sister for deceiving her, and herself for preparing the pyre.

Anna heard the noise, half-fainted with horror, then fearing the worst ran through the crowds, tearing her cheeks with her nails and beating her breast as she ran, calling aloud to her dying sister: 'Is this what it meant? You were deceiving me all along? Is this what that pyre had in store for me, and those altar fires? You have left me – but where shall I start my complaints? We did everything together; have you rejected me now as you die? You should have asked me to share your fate; the same painful thrust of the sword, the very same moment should have taken us off together. With my own hands I built this pyre, and loudly called on our gods – then you placed yourself on it when I wasn't there! That was cruel. Dearest sister, you have destroyed yourself, and me, as well as your people and state, and Carthage, your city. Give me water to wash her wounds; if any last breath still hovers on her lips, let me catch it on mine.'

As she was speaking she had reached the top of the pyre. She took her sister, near death, in her arms, and sobbed as she cradled her, drying the dark drops of blood with her dress.

Dido tried to raise her heavy eyes to meet Anna's once more, but fainted: the breath hissed through the wound in her breast. Three times she struggled to lift herself up, and propped herself on her elbow: three times she fell back on the bed. She turned her eyes to look for the light in the sky above her, found it, and sighed.

693–705   Juno at last sent Iris down to end Dido's agony.

It was then that Juno all-powerful, in pity for the length of

Dido's sufferings and the slow agony of her death, sent Iris down from Olympus to release her soul as it fought to get free from her body. Because she was dying an untimely, undeserved death, miserably, before it was due, set on fire by her sudden passion, Proserpina had not yet taken the tress of fair hair from her head that consigned her to Hell.[7] So Iris, with dew on her saffron wings, flew down through the sky, trailing a rainbow of countless colours as the sunlight caught her, and stood by Dido's head.

'This tress, now sacred to Dis, I take, as I am directed, and so set you free from your body.' As she spoke, with her right hand she cut off the hair: all the warmth fled from Dido's body, and her life passed away on the wind.

Notes to Book IV

1 **Orion** A constellation, whose setting in autumn was accompanied by stormy weather.
2 **Ceres ... Apollo ... Wine-God (Bacchus)** These were all connected both with marriages and the foundation of cities. Ceres gave men laws because the discovery of corn led to settled, organised life.
3 **entrails** The Romans believed that the future could be diagnosed from the entrails of animals sacrificed as victims by special priests called soothsayers.
4 **Saturn** He was identified with the Greek god Kronos, whose children included Jupiter, Juno, Ceres, Hades and Poseidon.
5 **the Daughters of Evening (Hesperides)** They guarded the golden apples given by Mother Earth to Juno on her marriage to Jupiter.
6 **Erebus** Son of Chaos: they are both gods of the Underworld. Diana has three forms – in the sky she is the moon, on earth the huntress, and below the earth Hecate, a goddess associated with witchcraft and terror. So the sorceress' prayer becomes all the more horrifying.
7 **tress ... that consigned her to Hell** Part of the ritual at sacrifices was to cut some of a victim's hair as a first offering; similarly when men die at their appointed time Proserpina herself cuts off a lock of hair. But she cannot do it for Dido, who has died before her appointed time, so she sends Iris to do it as a mark of her compassion.

Book V

After the drama of the love affair, and the tragedy of Dido's death, the action in Book V is quiet, as if to allow Aeneas to recover his composure, and perhaps some of his credibility as a hero and a leader. Much of the story centres on his men, and Aeneas is almost an observer rather than a participant. After leaving Carthage the ships are again blown to Drepanum in Sicily, where Aeneas' father had died the year before; Aeneas decides to hold funeral games in Anchises' honour on the anniversary of his death.

First there is a boat race between four of the ships; we have met all four captains briefly in earlier Books. Then in a keenly contested foot race there is an accusation of unfair tactics, and Aeneas has tactfully to calm down some raised tempers; two of the runners, Nisus and Euryalus, appear again, in a more tragic episode after the Trojans have reached Italy. In a brutal boxing match, Aeneas intervenes to save the loser from serious injury. An archery contest is followed by a riding display, given by Ascanius and other young Trojans, which is interrupted by an urgent message. The Trojan women, incited by Juno, and weary of constantly wandering over the Mediterranean, have set fire to the ships.

At this Aeneas almost loses heart. Jupiter reassures him with a rain-storm that extinguishes the flames, with the loss of only four of the ships. Some of the Trojans decide to remain in Sicily, but Aeneas is encouraged by a vision of his father to lead the others on towards Italy. Palinurus, his helmsman, is lost overboard.

Characters

Trojans
Aeneas, Anchises, Ascanius
In the boat race: Mnestheus, captain of *Shark*
       Sergestus, captain of *Centaur*
       Cloanthus, captain of *Scylla*
       Gyas, captain of *Chimaera*
       Menoetes, helmsman of *Chimaera*
In the foot race: Nisus, Euryalus, Salius, Diores, Helymus

1–103   On leaving Carthage the Trojans are caught in such a
violent storm that they have to run to Sicily for safety. They land
near Anchises' tomb and are welcomed by Acestes, the friendly
king with whom they had stayed on their previous visit. Aeneas
proclaims that funeral games will be held in honour of his father
in nine days' time.

104–243   The day they'd awaited so long had arrived, the ninth
day, with a fine clear dawn ushered in by the sun-god's horses.
The news of the games and the fame and prestige of Acestes had
brought out the sightseers from the country around; happy
crowds packed the beaches to watch Aeneas' men, some of them
ready to compete as well. First the prizes were displayed in the
centre of the field, for everyone to see, holy tripods, bright green
palm leaves to crown the winners, pieces of armour, clothes dyed
purple, and ingots of gold and silver. A fanfare on a trumpet
from a mound in the middle signalled the start of the games.

First was a boat race. Four ships chosen from the fleet had
been entered, equally matched in the power of their oars. The
swift ship *Shark*[1] and its lively crew were commanded by
Mnestheus – he was soon to become an Italian and pass on his
name to the Memmian family. Gyas commanded *Chimaera*, a
huge ship, the size of a city – its Trojan crew rowed in three tiers,
and three banks of oars rose together. Sergestus, after whom the
Sergian[2] family is named, was captain of the great ship *Centaur*,
and Cloanthus of dark-blue *Scylla* – he founded the Roman
family of Cluentius.

Far out at sea, facing the foaming shore, is a rock. Sometimes
in winter, when the stars are hidden by the dark nor'westers, it's
submerged and battered by swollen breakers, but in calm
weather it's a peaceful flat surface rising out of still water, where
the gulls love to perch and bask in the sunshine. On it Father
Aeneas had put a leafy green oak-branch as a mark for the
sailors, so they should know where to turn round and row the
long course back. The captains drew lots for position, then each
took his place on the stern, in brilliant clothes of purple and gold
(you could see them for miles!). The rest of the crews wore
garlands of poplar leaves, their bare shoulders shiny with oil
they'd rubbed in. They sat down on the benches, tensed arms on
oars, tensely awaiting the signal. Their hearts were leaping and
pounding with nervous excitement and the desperate desire to do
well. Loud and clear came the blast from the trumpet – in a flash

they all surged away from the start. The heavens rang with the bo'suns yelling the stroke, and the waves were churned into foam as they pulled the strokes through. Side by side they ploughed through the sea, and the surface peeled back as the prows knifed through it, and boiled round the oar-blades . . .

Amid all the excitement and noise, Gyas moves out in front of the others, pulling ahead: in second place was Cloanthus, with a better-trained crew, but the dead weight of their slow-moving craft held them back. Neck and neck behind them *Centaur* and *Shark* fought for third place; first *Shark* has it, then the great *Centaur* catches and passes her, and next they forge on together with their bows dead-level and their long keels furrowing the salt sea-water.

Now they were nearing the rock, and close to the turning-point, when Gyas, in the lead at half-way and looking like winning, yelled to his helmsman Menoetes: 'Why are you steering so far out to starboard? Steer in here! Hug the rock's edge! Let the oar-blades just graze it to port; the others can keep to deep water!'

But Menoetes was afraid of hidden rocks, and turned the bows out to the sea.

'You're off course! Where are you going?', called Gyas again. 'Head for the rocks, Menoetes!' Looking back at that moment he saw Cloanthus holding the inside course, and closing up fast. And Cloanthus just scraped through on his left, between the roaring rock-face and Gyas' ship, and suddenly shooting ahead he had rounded the rock and made his way into safe water.

Then a great surge of anger coursed through young Gyas' bones, and tears of frustration ran down his cheeks: forgetting his dignity, and the safety of his crew, he pitched the cautious Menoetes head first into the sea, a long fall from way up on the stern. Taking the tiller himself, helmsman and captain combined, and yelling encouragement to the men, he steered the boat round towards the shore. But Menoetes, heavy with age and weighed down by his soaking wet clothes, in the end only just struggled up from the bottom; he scrambled to the top of the rock, and sat down in the dry. The Trojans roared with laughter at the sight of him falling and swimming, and they burst out laughing again as he spewed up a flood of salt sea.

The last two, Sergestus and Mnestheus, were suddenly fired with the hope of passing Gyas as he lagged behind. Sergestus squeezed in front near the rock, but by no means completely clear, for *Shark*'s bows had a half-length overlap. Mnestheus ran down to the waist of his ship, coaxing the men on each side: 'Come on, men! You once fought with Hector; I chose you to be my comrades in the last hours of Troy – now rise to the oars! Now show the strength and guts you displayed in the African sandbanks, in the Ionian Sea, and the chasing waves of Cape Malea![3] I, Mnestheus, am not after first place any more, not fighting to win, though . . . But let victory go to those whom Neptune has chosen. But last place *would* be a disgrace! You must do better than that, my Trojans, and avoid such a dreadful defeat!'

They pulled with enormous effort, and the bronze stern trembled under their mighty strokes, and the sea slid by beneath them; their panting gasps for breath shook their parched throats and their bodies; rivers of sweat flowed all over them.

An accident brought Mnestheus' crew the honour he wanted. For Sergestus, in impatient excitement, steered his bows towards the rock, and coming up on the inside, without enough room, unluckily ran aground on an out-jutting reef. The rocks shook at the impact, oars grated and snapped on the sharp jagged edge, the bows smashed aground and stuck, high and fast. Up leaped the sailors, backed water with furious curses, got out the iron-tipped boat-hooks and sharp-pointed pikes, and fished in the swell for their broken oars.

But Mnestheus was pleased at this piece of good luck, and much more encouraged. Rowing flat out, and calling the winds to help him, he made for the sea sloping down to the shore, speeding over the open water. It was just like a dove, suddenly flushed from a cave where its nest and its sweet little nestlings are lodged in the cracks of the rock: scared out of its home, it skims over the fields with its wings clapping loudly, then cleaves a smooth path through the silent air, gliding on motionless wings. So Mnestheus and *Shark* cut a course down the final lap, as the ship flew on under its own momentum.

First she left Sergestus behind, struggling high up on the rock and then in the shallows, calling in vain for help, and learning to row with pieces of oars. Next she overtook Gyas and the massive *Chimaera*, which, deprived of its helmsman, soon fell behind. And now at the finish, only Cloanthus was left. Mnestheus went after him, wringing out the last ounce of strength to get close. Then the clamour really redoubled, as everyone roared on his chase, and the heavens re-echoed with their thunderous applause. One crew could not bear to lose the triumph that was theirs, the honour they'd almost won, and would mortgage their lives for glory. The others fed on success – they could do it because they believed that they could. Now Mnestheus had come up level, might even have snatched the prize, but Cloanthus stretched both hands over the sea, poured out prayers, and swore to abide by his promise: 'You gods, whose empire is Ocean, over whose waters we race, to fulfil this vow, on this very shore I will gladly lay a white bull on your altar; the salt waves shall receive its entrails, and streams of clear wine shall I pour.'

Deep down under the waves he was heard by the gods of the sea; and father Portunus himself, god of harbours, with his own great hand gave the vessel a push on its way; swifter than the south wind or the flight of an arrow, it flew in to land and came to rest deep in the harbour.

244–67   Aeneas presents the prizes to the first three, Cloanthus, Mnestheus and Gyas.

268–81   Sergestus arrives.

Now they had received their prizes and were proudly going off with their spoils ... when Sergestus was sighted: he had managed with considerable skill to pull his ship off that unfriendly rock; though he had lost some oars – one whole tier was right out of action – he was bringing her in, to hoots of derisive laughter. Often a snake is caught on the high road, and the bronze-shod wheel of a cart runs over its back, or an angry traveller smashes its head with a rock, and leaves it crushed and half-dead by the roadside. It wriggles and writhes in a futile attempt to escape: half of it raises its head, its eyes flashing anger, and hisses, but the other half, maimed by the wound, prevents it from getting away, though it twists and tangles itself into knots. That's how the handicapped vessel limped along – but then she made sail too, and came into harbour under full sail. Aeneas still gave Sergestus the prize for fourth place – he was glad that the ship was safe, and his friends were on shore.

282–314   The spectators now move off to a grassy running track in a valley forming a natural amphitheatre. There are many competitors for the foot race, including Nisus and Euryalus, Helymus, Salius and Diores. Aeneas announces the prizes for the first three.

315–61 After Aeneas' speech they went to their marks, the signal was given and they were off like a shot down the track, dashing along like a storm cloud. Then as soon as they came in sight of the finish Nisus got away from the rest, shooting into the lead, swifter than the winds or winged lightning. Next, but a long, long way back, Salius gave chase; another gap, then in third place Euryalus, with Helymus following close. Then they saw Diores, going like the wind, come up behind him, treading on Helymus' heels, then almost shoulder to shoulder. Had the course been longer he'd have slipped right past him, or at least left third place in doubt.

Now with the race nearly over they were wearily coming up to the finish, when Nisus unluckily slipped on a wet patch of blood: some bullocks had been sacrificed there, as it happened, and blood was spilt on the ground, soaking the green grass. It was here that, already triumphant at winning, the young man trod, lost his footing, staggered and fell face down in the filthy mess and the blood from the sacrifice. Even then he remembered his good friend Euryalus; he rose from the slippery patch, and threw himself in Salius' way. Salius was bowled right over, and lay flat out on the beaten track. Euryalus shot ahead, and thanks to his friend came first, flying in to rousing applause and cheers. Second was Helymus, and in third place Diores.

At this, Salius loudly appealed to the dense crowd in the huge amphitheatre and the lords in the front row, demanding to be given the prize of which he'd been robbed by a foul. But Euryalus had the crowd on his side – they liked his decent embarrassment, and no doubt his good looks made his success the more welcome. Diores, too, noisily supported him; though winning a place, he'd lose his third prize if Salius were awarded the first. Father Aeneas announced: 'The prizes are yours, men, don't worry; no one is changing the order. But let me show some sympathy for a friend – he didn't deserve to fall.' So saying he presented Salius with the skin of an enormous African lion, with a long shaggy mane and gold-painted claws.

Then Nisus said: 'If you have such prizes for losers, and sympathy for those who fall, what gift have you got for me? I deserve one, for I would have won first prize if I hadn't had the same bad luck as Salius.' As he was speaking he was showing his body and face, all foul from the liquid slime. Father Aeneas smiled at him, and ordered a shield to be brought . . . and gave an outstanding prize to this very special young man.

362–603   A boxing match follows, then an archery contest, won by Acestes, the Sicilian king. Next Ascanius and some other young Trojans give a riding display, with three groups of twelve riders galloping back and forth in an intricate pattern.

604–40   Through all this time the Trojan women, who were not allowed to watch the games, have been mourning Anchises, and bewailing their own misfortunes. Juno sends Iris down in an attempt to make sure that the Trojans shall not leave Sicily.

At this point in the games held in honour of Anchises, Fortune changed sides and broke faith with the Trojans. While, with these various contests, they were paying their respects at the tomb, Juno sent Iris down from heaven to the Trojan ships, breathing fair winds behind her. She had more tricks in store, for her long-standing resentment was not yet appeased. Iris sped down the curve of the rainbow with its countless colours, flying so fast that no one saw her. She sighted the enormous crowd, and flew down the beach till she spotted the deserted harbour, and the ships with no one on guard.

Some way away, on a lonely part of the shore by themselves, the women of Troy were weeping for the loss of Anchises, and gazing at the deep wide sea as they wept. 'We are weary of all this water, yet there's so much sea still to cross', they cried, one and all. They were sick of the sea and sailing, they longed for a city.

So Iris, no stranger to mischief-making, ran quickly amongst them; discarding the face and clothes of a goddess, she turned into Beroë, the old wife of Doryclus, who had once had family, name and children. It was in her likeness that Iris joined them: 'Poor women, what a pity the Greeks didn't drag us away and kill us under the walls of Troy! What an unlucky people we are! For what kind of death, I wonder, has Fortune kept us alive? It's seven years since Troy was destroyed, yet we're still wandering from land to land, past straits and unfriendly rocks, with only the stars to guide us, rolling in the waves of the ocean, in search of that elusive Italy. But the lands of Eryx[4] (isn't he Aeneas' brother?), and the hospitable King Acestes, are here. Who's going to stop us from building the walls of our city here, and giving ourselves a home? O Troy! O home-gods of Troy, why were you saved if no town will be called Troy again? Shall I not see a Simois or Xanthus[5] anywhere, the rivers that Hector knew? Come on! Help me to burn these accursed ships! For a vision of Cassandra, our own prophetess, appeared in a dream and handed me burning torches: "Look for Troy here," she said, "make your home here!" Now is the time to do something, we mustn't keep such important omens waiting! Here are four altars to Neptune – Neptune himself is providing the torches, and the courage to use them!'

641–63   Iris flings the first firebrand. The women hesitate at first, but when Iris reveals that she is a goddess they are seized by fury and set fire to the ships.

Even as she spoke she was the first to snatch up a deadly firebrand. Raising her right hand high, and gathering her strength, she whirled it around, and threw! The minds of the women were startled, and their senses were stunned. Then one of their number, the oldest, Pyrgo, the royal nurse of all Priam's numerous children, called out: 'This is not Beroë, ladies, this isn't Doryclus' Trojan wife! Look at her blazing eyes and beauty, the marks of divinity! Mark her proud bearing, that look, the tone of her voice, her walk! I only left Beroë myself a moment ago! She was unwell, and annoyed at being the only one not at the ceremony and unable to pay Anchises his proper respect.'

The women were in two minds at first, and angrily glared at the ships, torn between their own pitiful desire for the land they were in, and the call of the land promised by Fate. But then the goddess took off, spread her wings, and cut a huge rainbow curve as she flew away under the clouds. Amazed by this miraculous sign, in frenzied excitement they took up the cry, snatched fire from the hearths of the Trojan encampment, or else robbed the altars, throwing the greenery, kindling and firebrands at the ships. The Fire-God raged and rampaged through the benches, the oars, and the painted pinewood sterns.

664–75   When news of the fire reaches the games Ascanius gallops off and tries to bring the women back to sanity, then Aeneas and the others arrive.

676–99   The women run away in fright. When the Trojans are unable to put out the flames, Aeneas appeals to Jupiter either to send help, or to destroy them on the spot. A great storm does extinguish the fires.

But the women were scared, and scattered over the shore in every direction, stealthily making for the woods, or any caves in the rocks to hide in. They were ashamed to be seen after what they had done: but recovering from the madness that Juno had inspired, they came to their senses and recognised their menfolk. But that didn't make the flames or the fires lose their unquenchable strength: down in the moist timbers the tow still smouldered and gave off a thick slow smoke, and the dangerous heat spread down through the hulls, and was slowly consuming the keels. All the efforts of the men, the floods of water poured in, made no difference.

Then the good Aeneas ripped the cloak from his shoulders, stretched out his hands, and called on the gods for help: 'Almighty Jupiter, if you do not yet utterly loathe all the Trojans, if you still in your tender mercy have some regard for the sufferings of men, grant that our ships may escape the flames *now*. Save the frail hopes of Troy from destruction. If not, if I deserve no better, then blast us, the few that are left, down to Hell with your furious thunderbolt! Crush us with your right hand, *here and now!*'

He'd hardly stopped speaking before a cloudburst of rain poured down in a storm of unimaginable fury, and the mountains and plains of the earth trembled at the claps of thunder. Violent torrents of rain fell from every corner of the sky, and dense black clouds blew up from the south. The ships brimmed over with water and the half-burnt timbers were drenched, till all the fires were extinguished, and all except four of the ships were saved from destruction.

700–871   Aeneas, still disturbed by the disaster, wonders whether he should settle in Sicily after all. But he is advised that while *he* should go on, the weak and timid should be left behind.

Later, a vision of Anchises appears in a dream, and tells him to follow this advice and to sail on with the bravest of his men to Italy. He must find a prophetess called the Sibyl, who will take him down to the Underworld to meet Anchises, from whom Aeneas will learn of his own future and that of his descendants. Accordingly Aeneas marks out the site of the new town for the Trojans who are staying in Sicily, and his ships are repaired. Nine days later Aeneas sails sadly away.

Venus, afraid that Juno will cause yet another storm, asks Neptune to help bring Aeneas safely to the mouth of the Tiber. He promises to do so, at the cost of one Trojan life. When Aeneas observes the sea grow completely calm his confidence returns, and all the sails are spread to catch the favourable breezes. During the night the helmsman Palinurus falls asleep and is lost overboard, the one life that Neptune demands.

Notes to Book V

1 **Shark ... Chimaera ... Centaur ... Scylla** The four ships have the names of fabulous monsters. The word translated as Shark means some kind of sea-monster, possibly 'Leviathan'. The Chimaera was a three-part dragon, a lion in front, a serpent behind and a goat in the middle. Centaurs had the upper part of a human body, the lower part of a horse. Scylla had six heads. The ships would have had figure-heads resembling these creatures.

2 **Sergian family** Roman families were fond of tracing their names back to Trojan ancestors.

3 **Malea** The south-eastern promontory of the Greek Peloponnese, notorious for stormy seas.

4 **Eryx** The legendary king of a mountain in north-west Sicily; as a son of Venus, he was Aeneas' half-brother.

5 **Simois and Xanthus** Rivers near Troy.

Book VI

Aeneas and his followers sail through the Etruscan Sea, to the west of Italy, and land on the coast at Cumae. He consults the local prophetess, the Sibyl, and asks her help to visit his father in the Underworld. She tells him that he must first find in the woods the Golden Bough, which he must take down as a gift to Proserpina, the queen of the Underworld. When he has found it, Aeneas and the Sibyl make their way down through a cave near Lake Avernus. The first region they pass through is inhabited by abstract monsters, like Grief and Agony. They reach the river Acheron, where countless ghosts of people as yet unburied have to wait, unable to cross. But the Sibyl shows Charon the ferryman the Golden Bough, and he takes them over. After drugging the watchdog Cerberus they come to the Plains of Mourning, where they find all those who have died an early death. Here Aeneas sees and speaks to the ghost of Dido. They then pass by Tartarus, where sinners are punished, to Elysium, where Aeneas meets his father. Aeneas sees a throng of souls waiting, and Anchises explains how souls are reborn after purification. Among them he points out the souls of men who will be famous in Roman history. Then Aeneas and the Sibyl return to the real world above.

Characters

Sibyl, the name given to the priestesses of Apollo at Cumae, who were thought to be skilled in prophecy. The collection of their oracles, known as the Sibylline Books, played an important part in Roman religion

Charon, ferryman of the River Styx

Aeneas and his father Anchises

Places

Cumae, a town on the coast of Italy, 100 miles south of modern Rome

Avernus, a lake near Cumae, close to the entrance of Hades. The name Avernus is also sometimes used for the Underworld itself. The lake was thought to be fed by the river Acheron, flowing up from the Underworld. Other rivers there were Styx, Cocytus, Lethe and Phlegethon

The Underworld was divided into two parts: Tartarus, where

sinners were punished after death, and Elysium, where good people enjoyed a full and pleasant 'life'

 1–13   On landing at Cumae Aeneas goes at once to the temple of Apollo in search of the Sibyl.

With a tearful farewell for his helmsman Aeneas sailed on at full tilt till at last the fleet came smoothly to shore at Cumae. They turn the prows to the sea, then make the ships fast with the firm grip of hooked anchors; the curved sterns form a kind of decorative fringe to the beach. The young Trojans eagerly leap down to the shore, the Italian shore. Some go searching for the seeds of fire that are hidden in veins of flint. Others raid the forests and the wild beasts' lairs for wood, and point to the rivers they find. But Aeneas remembers his duty and makes for the heights, for Apollo's shrine that protects them, and the huge cave where the awesome Sibyl lives like a hermit. Apollo gives her great understanding, and the power to look deep into the future. Soon they approach the grove of Diana, and the golden temple there.

14–41   An account of the temple's history follows. The Trojans are gazing in awe at the legendary scenes that are carved on the temple doors, when the Sibyl arrives and recalls Aeneas to his duty.

42–76   The Trojans reach a huge cavern from which the oracles are given. The Sibyl is gradually possessed by the influence of Apollo, and orders Aeneas to pray for what he wants.

In the side of the hill at Cumae is a huge cave hollowed out of the rock. It has a hundred mouths and a hundred wide roads leading into it – when the Sibyl gives answers a hundred voices rush out. They had come to the entrance when, 'It is time to ask for your fate', cried the Sibyl. 'Here, here's the god!' Suddenly, as she was speaking in front of the doors, her face and her colour changed, her hair blew about in disorder. Quicker and quicker she breathed; her heart swelled wildly in frenzy; she seemed to grow larger, with a voice no longer human, for the god was now nearer and his spirit possessed her. 'You are slow, Trojan Aeneas, too slow, in uttering your vows and prayers: until you do, the great mouths of this home of the god shall be spellbound, and not yawn open.' She spoke and fell silent.

An icy shudder of fear ran through the Trojans' bones, hard though they were, and Aeneas poured out prayers from the depths of his noble soul. 'Phoebus,[1] who always took pity on Troy in her grievous sorrows, who guided the arrow from Paris' hand into the body of Achilles; it was you who brought me through so many seas encircling the great land-masses, through distant Numidian tribes, past Africa's northern coast-lands. At long last we have reached the elusive Italian shore – let Troy's ill luck follow this far, but no further. You gods and goddesses all, to whom Troy and the great fame of Troy were offensive, now it is right for you too to spare us Trojan people.

'And you, most holy Sibyl, you who foresee the future – I am only asking for the kingdom my destiny owes me – grant that we Trojans may settle in Latium, with our far-travelled, hard-driven Trojan gods. Then shall I build a temple of solid marble to Phoebus and Diana, and set up a festival in Phoebus' honour. For you, O priestess, there shall be in my kingdom a magnificent shrine: here I shall place your oracles, those secrets of fate revealed to my people. I shall ordain noble priests to serve you, dear lady. Yet do not commit your sayings to leaves, lest they become playthings for the bustling winds to scatter. Speak them aloud, I beg you.'

77–97   The Sibyl, now in the cave and inspired by Apollo, promises that the Trojans shall rule in Italy, though at a high cost.

But the prophetess had not yet given in to Phoebus; like an unbroken horse she fought back wildly in the cave, in the hope of throwing him off. But he wore out her foaming mouth all the more, tamed her fierce spirit, and broke her with rigid control. And now the hundred huge doors of the cave, of their own accord, flew open and carried the Sibyl's reply through the air: 'You have won your way, at long last, through the fearsome dangers of the sea – yet worse await you on land. The Trojans *shall* come to rule in Lavinium[2] (no need any more to worry about that), but shall wish they had not done so. I see wars, dreadful wars, and the Tiber afoam with torrents of blood . . . Juno will give the Trojans no rest. There's not a tribe or town in Italy that, in desperate need, you will not approach for help. The cause of such great harm for the Trojans will again be a foreign bride,[3] again an alien marriage. But never give in to misfortunes – go to meet them more boldly still, in whatever way your fortune allows you. And the first helping hand on the road to safety will come, where you'd least expect it, from a city of Greeks.'

98–123   The Sibyl recovers. Aeneas begs her to show him the way to the Underworld so that he may meet his father.

In such words did the Sibyl sing out from her sanctuary the terrifying riddles; her voice boomed out of the cave as she wrapped up her truths in mystery. And Phoebus tugged on the reins as she raved, and twisted the goad in her heart. As soon as her madness abated and her delirious voice fell quiet, Aeneas bravely began: 'None of these troubles that face me seem unexpected or new. I've foreseen them all: in my mind I've gone through them already. One thing I ask. Here, it is said, is the gateway to Hell, and the dark grim marsh where Acheron flows up from the Underworld. I hope to have the good fortune to meet, face to face, my dear father. Open the sacred doors and show me the way. I brought him out on my shoulders here, through the flames and the countless spears that pursued us, saved him from the thick of the enemy. He came with me on my journey through sea after sea, and, weak though he was, endured all the threats of ocean and sky, ordeals beyond the strength and the normal risks of old age. It was he who begged me, told me, to come to your home and make this request. So, kind lady, take pity on father and son, for you have the power to do anything; it was with very good reason that Hecate[4] put you in charge of the groves of Avernus. If Orpheus[5] could go down to get his wife back with only the tuneful strings of his lyre to rely on . . . if Theseus and great Hercules – but why mention them? I too am descended from great Jupiter.'

124–48   The Sibyl tells him that he must find the Golden Bough, to take as a gift to Proserpina (wife of Dis, ruler of the Underworld).

These were the prayers he made as he clung to the altar; and the prophetess began her reply: 'O Trojan son of Anchises, who have the blood of the gods in your veins, the way down to Avernus is easy; the gates of the dark world of Dis lie open by night and by day. But to retrace your steps, to make your way back to the air above, that is an uphill task, that is a struggle. A few, sons of gods, have succeeded – either because of Jupiter's affection and favour or through their own exceptional prowess. All the way down there are woods, and the river Cocytus winds its dark coils round like a snake. But if the desire in your mind is so strong, this passion to cross the waters of Styx twice over, to see black Tartarus twice, if you're set on this crazy ordeal, then listen to what you must do first.

'Concealed in a shady tree is a bough; it is golden, and so are the leaves on its tough pliant stem. It is said to be sacred to Proserpina. The whole wood protects it, tucked away in the gloom and shade of a valley. Now, no one may go down to the earth's secret places until he has plucked from the tree this golden-haired growth. For Proserpina in all her beauty has decreed that it must be brought as a gift to herself. When one bough is pulled away another grows in its place; it too will be golden, and the leaves that sprout on the branch will be of the selfsame metal. Keep your eyes up high as you search, and pluck it with reverent hand when you've found it. It will come away by itself, easily, without any fuss, if the Fates intend you to go. If they don't, all your strength will not get it for you, hard steel won't pry it loose.'

149–89 Aeneas leaves the cave and returns to the beach, where he finds that one of his men has been killed. To get wood for the funeral pyre they go into the forest, and Aeneas despondently voices a vain hope of seeing the bough.

190–211 The words are hardly out of his mouth before two doves chance to come gliding down from the sky, right in front of his eyes, and touch down on the bright green turf. Recognising that these birds[6] are his mother's, the great hero joyfully prays: 'Lead me, if there's a way, and steer your flight through the air to the part of the wood where the fertile soil is shaded by that precious bough. And you, my mother divine, don't let me down at this critical moment.' So saying he stood quite still, to see what signs they might give, and in what direction they'd go.

They flew ahead, pecking at food as they went, but never so far that those who followed lost sight of them. Then, when they came to the mouth of foul-smelling Lake Avernus, they soared up swiftly, planed through the bright-clear air, came to rest where he'd prayed they would, on this composite tree, where a different colour gleamed, a hint of gold in the branches. In the depths of winter in the woods mistletoe still grows with fresh leaves, though its roots aren't its own, encircling the smooth dark trunks with its bright yellow growth. The gold leafy bough on the evergreen oak looked just like that, as its gold-foil gently clinked in the breeze. Aeneas seized it at once, eagerly snapped it off, though not all that easily, and carefully carried it back to the home of the Sibyl.

212–35 They all return to the beach for the funeral of the dead man.

236–63 Aeneas and the Sibyl prepare to enter the Underworld.

Next Aeneas hastened to follow the Sibyl's instructions. There was a monstrous and deep jagged cave, yawning wide open, screened by a murky lake and the gloom of the forest. No birds could wing their way safely above it, so lethal the vapour that poured from its sombre jaws and rose to the vault of heaven. First, the priestess brought to this place four black bullocks. She poured wine on their foreheads, then snipped off the tops of the hairs growing between their horns[7] and threw them into the fire as the first offering, calling aloud upon Hecate, mistress of heaven and hell. Others slit the victims' throats with their knives, and caught the warm blood in bowls. Aeneas used his sword to sacrifice a black-fleeced lamb to Night, the mother of the Furies,[8] and to Earth, her great sister, and a barren heifer to Proserpina. Then he built temporary altars to Dis, the king of the Underworld, and put on their flames whole carcasses of bulls, and poured rich olive oil over their burning entrails.

That was all done in the night, but then on the threshold of day, at the first glimmer of sunlight, the ground underfoot seemed to moan, the wooded hill-tops started moving, and in the half-light the howling of dogs proclaimed that Hecate herself was coming.

'Those that are not allowed here must go right away,' cried the Sibyl; 'go back, out of the wood. But Aeneas, draw your sword and go forward. Now you need all your courage and drive.' Without another word she plunged, in her ecstasy, right into the cave; and Aeneas resolutely marched stride for stride, by her side.

264–81   Virgil begs permission from the gods of the Underworld to reveal their secrets, then starts his description.

You gods who rule the souls of the dead, you unspeaking shades, and Chaos, and Phlegethon, river of fire, O silent world of night; grant me the right to tell what I've heard, grant me your divine consent to reveal the secrets hidden in darkness and depths of earth!

Cloaked in the lonely darkness of night they set off through the desolate empty realms of Dis. It was just like walking in a forest by the feeble light of a fitful moon, when Jupiter has hidden the sky in shadow, and the blackness of night steals the colour of things. Just by the porch at the mouth of Hell were the lairs of Grief and vengeful Anxiety; there dwelt pallid Diseases, gloomy Old Age, and Fear, the Hunger that leads men to crime, Poverty in all its ugliness, and the horrible shapes of Suffering and Death. There too was Sleep, Death's brother, sinful Pleasures and, right on the threshold, War, the bringer of Death. In iron cells were the Furies, and insane Civil War whose hair, formed of snakes, was tied with a blood-stained band.

282–94   Virgil goes on to describe other monsters at the mouth of hell, like Centaurs and Gorgons.

295–332   Aeneas and the Sibyl move forward to the river Acheron. (It flows into the Cocytus, which in turn joins the Styx.)

From here the road leads to the deadly waters of Acheron. Here is a boiling swamp, with a great swirling whirlpool of slime belching up sludge into Cocytus. A horrible ferryman, named Charon, looks after the river crossing. He's appallingly dirty, and his chin is covered with an unkempt long grey beard; his eyes dart fire, and a grimy cloak trails in a tangle down from his shoulders. He punts the boat out with a pole, unaided, then sees to the sails, taking the dead across in his rust-coloured ferry. Old he may be, but a god's old age is green and sprightly.

Down to the bank to meet him rushed a whole crowd, of mothers and husbands, courageous heroes finished with life, boys and unmarried girls, and young men laid on the pyre while their parents looked on. They were as numerous as the leaves that fall from the woodland trees at the first chill of autumn, or as the birds flocking in to land from the sea, when winter drives them across the ocean to a sunnier climate. They stood there, begging to be first to cross over, stretching out their hands as if longing to touch the far bank. These or those the sour old ferryman took, but others he shoved aside, and kept them well back from the bank.

Aeneas was amazed, and upset by all the commotion. 'Tell me, O Sibyl, what is the meaning of this crowd by the river? What do the spirits want? What decides which of them should turn sadly away, and which should row over those murky waters?'

The aged priestess briefly replied: 'Son of Anchises, and true-born child of the gods, you are looking at the rivers and swamps of Hell . . . This crowd that you see is made up of those who are helpless, unburied. The ferryman is Charon. Those who do cross the river have been given burial. But none of them can be taken over those roaring streams and menacing banks till their bones have been laid to rest. They wander for a hundred years, flitting around these shores – only then are they given permission to visit again the waters they long to cross.'

Anchises' son stood still, thinking it out, with pity in his heart for their unfair fate.

333–83 They see some of Aeneas' companions who have died on their travels, including Palinurus, his helmsman.

384–416 Despite Charon's unwillingness to take them, they cross the Styx.

So then they continued their journey and approached the river. Now, from out on the water, the ferryman saw them making their way through the silent woods and stepping towards the bank. Before they could say a word he shouted aggressively at them: 'Whoever you are there, carrying weapons and coming towards my river, halt! Stay where you are, and tell me why you have come. This is the land of the Dead, of Sleep and slumbrous Night. It's forbidden to ferry the living across in the Stygian boat. It was a grim day for me when Hercules came, and I took him across the water. Theseus and Pirithous too I should have refused, even though they were sons of gods, and irresistibly strong. Hercules wanted to put a leash on Cerberus, and forcibly dragged the poor frightened beast away from the throne of our king – the other two tried to enter his bedroom and kidnap our mistress.'

The priestess briefly dismissed his protest. 'Calm down, there's no such treachery here! These weapons don't mean violence. That huge watchdog in his cave can go on barking for ever, to scare those bloodless ghosts. Proserpina can keep house for her uncle, no one's going to assault her. This is Aeneas of Troy, who is famed for devotion to duty as much as for fighting. He has come to meet his father in the deepest shades of Hell. If the sight of such devotion leaves you entirely unmoved, well, you have to recognise *this*!' And she showed him the golden bough she'd concealed in her cloak.

That was all she needed to say, for the anger in Charon's heart at once cooled down. He gazed in awe at the holy branch which fate had decreed must be given – he'd seen it before, in the distant past – then turned his sombre craft round and headed back to the bank. There were other ghosts already seated along the benches, but he pitched them out and cleared the gangway, then welcomed Aeneas aboard. The old clinker boat groaned beneath the weight of his massive frame, and water poured in through the cracks. But he got the hero and priestess across in the end, and landed them safe in the coarse grass of an ugly mud-bank.

417–25 The priestess deals with Cerberus.

Across the month of a cave lay the huge body of Cerberus, as he

101

made the Underworld ring with the howls from his three throats. The priestess saw that the snakes on his neck were already beginning to bristle, so she threw him a titbit of honey and corn, doctored with sedative drugs. Crazy with hunger the animal opened all three months and gobbled down what she had thrown him. The great body flopped to the floor of the cave, sprawling from wall to wall. Aeneas sprang past the unconscious watchdog into the entrance, swiftly leaving the bank to which no one ever returns.

> 426–39   They see first the haunts of those who died before their time (there are five groups of them in all).

At once they heard crying, the loud wailing and sobbing of infant ghosts; right at the threshold of life a black day had stolen their share of the pleasure of life, and torn them away from their mothers' breasts, sending them down to a premature death.

Next are the men sentenced to death on a trumped-up charge. Here they are granted an impartial jury selected by lot, to determine their fate. President of the court is Minos,[9] who summons a panel of ghosts, and examines the charges made against then on earth.

Next place is held by those sad creatures who violently killed themselves: they had done nothing wrong, but threw life away because they hated their lives on earth. How glad they would be now, even suffering hardship and poverty, to be back in the world above! But the Law of the gods forbids it, and the frightful swamp with its dismal waters bars their escape, while the Styx, flowing round nine times, confines them.

> 440–76   The fourth group of the untimely dead includes Dido.

Not far from here can be seen the so-called Plains of Mourning, spreading in every direction. Those who have been cruelly consumed by the wasting disease of merciless love hide in a myrtle forest, haunting its secret walks. But even in death there's no cure for their love. Among a number of legendary lovers, Dido of Carthage, her wound unhealed, was wandering through the great wood. When she came near, the Trojan recognised her thin ghostly form in the shadows – like someone who sees, or imagines he sees, a new moon rise through the clouds. His eyes filled with tears, and in soft loving tones he said: 'Poor Dido, so the news that reached me was true, that you had died and made an end to your life with the sword? Oh god, was I the cause of your death? I swear by the stars, by the gods above, by whatever is sacred in the world below, it was not of my own free will, my queen, that I left your land. The same commands of the gods which are driving me now through these shadows, through this drear and desolate place, this pitch black night – it was them that drove me away. I could not refuse. I never believed that, by going away, I'd bring you such awful distress. Please wait! Don't walk away and leave me! Who are you running away from? This is the last chance to talk that Fate will allow us.'

With these words Aeneas tried to soften her angry heart and the scornful look in her eyes: but the only tears were his own. She turned aside and kept her eyes fixed on the ground; her expression was no more changed by what he had started to say than if she were carved from flint or marble. At last she swept away, and hating him still, fled to the darkness of the wood where her former husband Sychaeus answered her sorrows, giving her love for love. Yet Aeneas was still stricken by her unfair plight, and followed her till she was gone with eyes full of tears and pity.

477–554   The fifth group contains the ghosts of dead soldiers, both Trojan and Greek. They see the appallingly mutilated spirit of Deiphobus, who had married Helen after the death of Paris. He tells Aeneas that on the night when Troy was sacked Helen had stealthily let Menelaus into her house to take dreadful vengeance on the sleeping Deiphobus. The Sibyl interrupts them to tell Aeneas that they must hurry on.

They come to a fork in the road. The path to the right leads to Elysium, where they will find the ghosts of those who lived good and innocent lives. The path to the left goes to Tartarus; Aeneas looks down the path and sees a great walled castle, surrounded by a river of fire. An iron tower, by the door, rears high into the air.

555–84   The Sibyl tells Aeneas about the sinners in Tartarus, and their punishments.

On the iron tower sits Tisiphone, one of the Furies, wrapped in a blood-stained cloak. Day and night, never sleeping, she keeps watch at the entrance. From inside the walls groans could be heard, the savage crack of the whip, and the clanking of iron as chains were dragged by. Aeneas stopped in terror, listening aghast to the noise. 'What sort of crimes were those? Priestess, tell me, how are they punished? What is that awful wailing rising into the air?'

The Sibyl began: 'Famous leader of Trojans, no innocent person may set foot inside the door of the Damned. But when Hecate put me in charge of Avernus she told me about the punishments that the gods hand out, and took me to see everything. Here Rhadamanthus rules, most strictly. He listens to crimes committed, and issues a stern rebuke. He forces confessions from villains who rejoiced in escaping detection on earth: but retribution comes when they're dead, so there's no point in postponing it. At once the avenging Fury, Tisiphone, armed with a whip, pounces upon the guilty and beats them, shaking dread snakes in their faces, then calls on the cruel pack of her sisters to join her.

'Then, on screeching hinges, the dreaded gates swing open to let them in. You've seen the sentry who sits at the entrance – what a dreadful sight as she guards the door! – but posted inside is something even more savage, the monstrous Hydra, with fifty dark throats agape! Then Tartarus itself yawns open, a chasm stretching down into darkness twice as far as the view up to the top of Olympus for a man on earth. Here the old gods, the Titans,[10] children of Earth, writhe at the bottom of the pit where they were hurled by a thunderbolt. Here, too, I have seen the twin sons of Aloeus,[11] who tried with their bare hands to tear down the heavens and push Jupiter down from his throne up there . . .'

> 585–600   The Sibyl's list of such mythological sinners who have challenged the gods in some way continues, to conclude with one of the grimmest penalties.

'I could see Tityos, another child of the great Earth-mother (he assaulted Leto, the mother of Phoebus!). His body was spread over nine full acres; a monstrous vulture gnawed at his undying liver with cruel hooked beak, and rummaged for food in his guts, a rich source of torment; it had taken up residence deep in his chest, never giving him rest, for his entrails keep growing again.'

608–27   The Sibyl now turns from mythological sinners to mortals.

'Here too are those who, when they lived, hated their brothers, or struck at their parents; some defrauded dependants with a tissue of lies: some sat tight on the fortunes they'd made (there were hundreds of these), never giving their families a penny. Others were killed for adultery, or fought in treasonable wars, or dared to lie to their masters. All these are imprisoned here, to wait for their punishment. The form the punishment takes, the degree of severity, is almost too harsh to mention: some have to roll vast rocks, and others hang from the spokes of a wheel to which they are tied . . . Here's one who sold his country for gold, and gave it a ruthless dictator. This one made laws, and unmade them, for money. That one broke into his daughter's bedroom for illegal intercourse. They all dared a dreadful crime, and succeeded in doing it. Had I a hundred tongues, a hundred mouths and a voice of iron, I could never describe all the types of crime or run through the list of punishments.'

628–64   They move on, make the formal presentation of the Golden Bough, then take the right-hand path to Elysium.

The ancient priestess of Phoebus paused, then spoke again: 'But come now, you must step out, finish what you have started and deliver your offering. We must hurry; I can see the walls that were forged in the Cyclopes' furnace, and the arching gateway in front of us, where we were told to place the gift for Proserpina.' Side by side they walked through the shadows, covered the ground between, and came up to the gates. Aeneas was first to the entrance, where he sprinkled himself with fresh water, and hung the Bough on the door-post in front of him.

   Now that they'd completed their task and given their offering to Proserpina, they arrived at the Happy Places, the lovely green lawns of the Groves of Good Fortune, and the homes of the Blest.

105

Here the air is more generous, and covers the plain in a dazzling light: they have a sun and stars of their own. Some of the spirits are limbering up on the grass of the fields, or wrestling and fighting in the golden sand of the ring, all in sport. Others are stamping to the beat of a dance and chanting a chorus aloud . . . Orpheus is there in his long white robe to accompany the dance on the seven strings of his lyre, using his fingers and an ivory plectrum. Here are the ancient descendants of Teucer, a most handsome generation of heroes born in happier times: amongst them Dardanus, founder of Troy.

Aeneas, from some way off, was admiring the arms of these heroes, and their chariots standing idle. Their spears were stuck in the ground, their horses were grazing over the plain, unharnessed. All the pleasure that the heroes had found while alive in their weapons and chariots, the care they had taken in tending their well-groomed horses, followed them beyond the grave, unaltered.

Then he caught sight of some others, to left and right, who were picnicking on the grass, and singing a joyful hymn in a fragrant coppice of bay trees, from which a spring flowed in full flood to the world above. Gathered here were those who had, while on earth, been wounded in defence of their country, or had been saintly priests or poets of true goodness, whose songs were fit for Apollo, and men who had improved our lives by their skills and discoveries, or whose kindness to others had left an undying memory.

665–78   The Sibyl asks them where they can find Aeneas' father.

679–702   They find Anchises inspecting the souls which are to be born again.

In the depths of a cool green valley Anchises was reviewing the spirits confined there who were about to return to the world above, walking past them in careful scrutiny. He happened at that moment to be holding a roll-call of all his line, his dear descendants, taking stock of their fates and fortunes, characters and deeds. He suddenly saw Aeneas hurrying towards him across the grass, and eagerly held out his arms. Tears poured from his eyes, and he burst out: 'Have you really arrived at last?

Your father could rely on the love of his son to complete that difficult journey! Now I can look on your face, and talk, and hear your familiar voice! This is what I worked out and kept thinking would happen, as I crossed off the days. My anxious hopes have all come true! After a journey over so many seas and lands, welcome, son, welcome! What a difficult, dangerous journey! I was terrified you'd come to some harm at Carthage!' .

Aeneas answered: 'It was your worried phantom, father, appearing to me so often, that forced me to come to this place which is now your home. Our ships are safe at anchor in the Etruscan sea. Now give me your hand to hold, father, please don't draw away!' The tears poured down his face as he spoke. Three times he tried to put his arms round his father's neck, and three times the phantom slipped through his clutching hands, like a breath of wind or a fleeting dream.

> 703–23 Aeneas sees a great crowd of souls, and Anchises tells
> him what they are doing.

And now in a side-valley Aeneas saw the rustling trees of a half-hidden wood, where the river Lethe drifts past some quiet resting-places. Along its banks was flitting a numberless congregation, as bees on a fine summer day flit from flower to flower in the meadows, and swarm round the banks of white lilies as the whole field hums with their noise. This sudden sight startled Aeneas and, puzzled, he asked the reason, and what was the name of the river, and who were the crowds of people swarming along the banks.

'Those are the souls,' said his father, 'which are destined to have a second body on earth. They are drinking the waters of Lethe, which dispels all their former cares – the past is forgotten for ever. I've long been wanting to tell you all this, to show you in person my own descendants, to describe them one by one, to make you rejoice with me all the more at the finding of Italy.'

'Father, must we really believe that some souls soar upwards from here, and return once more to dull human bodies? What morbid desire for the light do these poor things have?'

'I'll tell you,' Anchises answered, 'to relieve all your doubts.'

724–51   Anchises explains that everything in the Universe is stirred into life by Mind. The origin of Mind is fire, and all living things have a spark of it in them. These souls are corrupted by contact with the body, and so must be purified with wind, water or fire. They then spend 1,000 years in Elysium before being returned to living bodies. The whole process is repeated till the Wheel of Time is complete. A few specially virtuous souls, like Anchises, may, after one life, stay in Elysium.

752–66   Anchises now points out the souls of the men who will make Rome great.

When he had finished, Anchises led Aeneas and the Sibyl into the thick of the murmuring assembly of souls. He chose a mound from which he could view the long line in front of him, and identify each one's face as they passed. 'Listen carefully now, as I tell you your destiny, and describe the glory in store for the children of Troy, the grandsons to come from your Italian marriage, the famous souls that will one day inherit our name. That young man there – do you see? – leaning on an untipped spear, has been allotted the next move into the light; he'll be the first to be born on earth with Italian and Trojan blood mixed. He'll be called Silvius, an Alban name. He'll be the last of your children, born late in your ripe old age. His mother, your wife Lavinia, will rear him in sylvan surroundings, to be a king and father of kings. It is his descendants, our family, who shall rule in Long Alba.

767–846   As Anchises points out the souls of future men as they pass by in succession, he describes a sort of pageant of Roman history. Grandson of the last king of Alba will be Romulus, the founder of Rome. Augustus, emperor in Virgil's time, is shown next: he will rule the Roman empire at its greatest, in a second golden age. He is followed by the other early kings of Rome, and famous men of the early republic. Then Julius Caesar and Pompey, and next a throng of other Romans who will win fame for their achievements in peace or war. Then Anchises goes on to sum up the greatness of Rome.

847–53   'Other peoples will, I am sure, be better at moulding breathing figures in bronze, and shaping lifelike features in marble. Others will speak more eloquently, and map out the movements of planets and predict when stars will rise. But, Romans, you, with your empire, must rule other people, never forget it. Your skills will be these; to crush the arrogant with war, show mercy to the vanquished and stamp civilisation on a world at peace.'

> 854–901 Anchises ends his description of the souls waiting to be born with an account of the sad death of Augustus' young nephew Marcellus. (Marcellus, who died in 23 BC, was deeply mourned by the Roman world, and his mother burst into tears when Virgil read this passage to her and Augustus.) Last, Aeneas hears briefly from his father of the wars he will have to fight in Italy, then immediately leaves the Underworld with the Sibyl, and returns to his ships.

Notes to Book VI

1 **Phoebus** Another name for Apollo: his sister was Diana.
2 **Lavinium** The town that Aeneas was to build in Latium.
3 **a foreign bride** The first foreign bride to cause the Trojans harm was Helen.
4 **Hecate** Queen of ghosts, often associated with Diana.
5 **Orpheus** Only a few living men were allowed to visit the Underworld. Orpheus' attempt to rescue his wife Eurydice is described in Book IV of Virgil's *Georgics*. One of Theseus' many legendary adventures was, with his friend Pirithous, an attempt to kidnap Proserpina. For this crime he was imprisoned in Hades till rescued by Hercules.
6 **these birds** The dove was sacred to Venus.
7 **hairs ... between their horns** To cut off some of the hair of a victim was part of the ritual of sacrifices. (Compare Book IV, note 7.)
8 **Furies** The Furies, Allecto, Megaera and Tisiphone, were spirits of punishment and vengeance.
9 **Minos** He, Rhadamanthus and Aeacus were judges of the dead, appointed to this position as a result of their just lives on earth. Rhadamanthus was also ruler of Elysium.
10 **Titans** The twelve Titans, children of Mother Earth, rebelled against Jupiter and were destroyed.
11 **the twin sons of Aloeus** These were Otus and Ephialtes: they piled Mount Ossa on Mount Pelion, and Mount Olympus on top of both, in an attempt to reach heaven and attack Jupiter.

Central Italy

Book VII

After the visit to the Underworld which forms the almost
religious climax to Aeneas' long voyage, Book VII introduces the
second half of Aeneas' story. Virgil's theme in this half of the
Aeneid is the start of Roman history, the grim series of battles
that Aeneas must fight against the various peoples who will, in
time, join his Trojans to become the Romans. Only when he has
won the war can he found his new city. But first we have to meet
the opposing forces, and to learn the reasons for the war. Just as
Juno in Book I persuaded Aeolus to rouse a fierce storm to wreck
the Trojans' fleet, so now she uses the Fury, Allecto, to rouse the
powers of Hell against them.

❦ ❦ ❦ ❦

Aeneas sails north from Cumae, and lands by the mouth of the
river Tiber. Virgil then rapidly explains that the country of
Latium is ruled by the aged King Latinus. His only child,
Lavinia, has many fine princes wanting to marry her, but the
favourite is Turnus, prince of the Rutuli, a neighbouring tribe: he
is also the man that Latinus' wife Amata wants as her son-in-law.
But Latinus is warned by omens to consult the oracle of his
father, Faunus, who tells him that Lavinia must not marry a
native prince, for she is fated to become the wife of a foreigner and
the mother of a race which will make the world its empire.

On landing the Trojans have a meal, and Aeneas becomes sure
that at last this is the land which is meant to be theirs. Next
morning, after a short reconnaissance, he starts to build a
military camp on the coast, while sending a hundred
ambassadors to Latinus to ask for peace.

Latinus welcomes them: he says that he knows who they are,
and recalls that Dardanus, founder of Troy, was born in Latium.
The ambassadors ask for a small piece of land to build a city, and
hand over the gifts sent by Aeneas. Latinus realises that this must
be the foreigner whom his daughter will marry, and promises
both peace, and his daughter as a bride, if Aeneas will come in
person to confirm the treaty.

At this point Juno, begrudging the Trojans' prospect of
success, sends the Fury, Allecto, to destroy their hopes of peace.
How she does so is told in the following extract.

In the general war-fever that Allecto arouses, Latinus refuses
his people's demand that he open the Gates of War in the temple
of Janus, so Juno herself breaks them open. There follows a list of
the tribes which gather to oppose the Trojans.

Characters

Gods
Juno
Allecto, one of the Furies

Trojans
Iulus, Aeneas' son

Italians
Latinus, king of the Laurentines, whose capital city was Lauren-
    tum, and ruler of Latium
Amata, his wife
Lavinia, his daughter
Tyrrhus, his huntsman
Silvia and Almo, daughter and son of Tyrrhus
Turnus, prince of the Rutuli, whose capital was at Ardea

 293–304   At the sight of Aeneas and the Trojans settling down
happily in Latium, Juno bursts into an angry tirade.

'Ugh! Those loathsome Trojans! Their destiny is at odds with
the destiny of me and mine. Did they fall dead on the plains of
Troy? In defeat could they be defeated? Were they burnt to ashes
in the flames of their city? No! Not they! They found their way to
escape right through the flames and the enemy swords. So I must
suppose that my divine power was finally exhausted and useless.
Was I through with hating and ready for peace? On no! When
they fled from Troy I hounded them savagely over the waves,
and wasted no chance to oppose them, with all the power of sea
and sky. But what good to me were Scylla,[1] Charybdis and the
African sandbanks? The Trojans have come to the haven they
wanted in the broad Tiber's waters, safe from the Ocean, and
from me!'

308–40   Juno decides that she must seek help to ruin the
Trojans.

'I can make myself felt as Jupiter's wife, I've stuck at nothing a poor goddess could think of, I've tried each and every trick, yet still I've been beaten by Aeneas. Well, if my own powers have now lost their strength, I won't mind asking for help, wherever it can be found. If I can't get heaven to help me, I'll stir up hell! I cannot stop Aeneas from winning his kingdom in Latium, or prevent his marriage to Lavinia. So be it: Fate has decided. Yet I *am* permitted to postpone, to delay his success, and to ruin the peoples of both these kings. Their lives will pay for the cost of uniting their families! Lavinia's dowry will be Italian and Trojan blood, her bridesmaid the goddess of war!'

With this dread promise she sped down to earth, horrific. From the darkness of hell where the dread Furies live, she summoned Allecto, maker of grief, who delights in the misery of war, in treachery, anger, and vicious dishonesty. Even her own father, Pluto, hates her, and her sisters in hell also hate the awful Allecto, so many the forms she assumes, so dreadful the shapes, so numerous the serpents that form her black hair! So Juno spoke to her, sharpening her temper with pointed words.

'Do me this service, O virgin goddess of night, a deed after your own heart, to free my worship and name from the risk of contempt or damage, to prevent the Trojans from inveigling Latinus into accepting this marriage and settling themselves in Italy. You have the power to set the closest of brothers at loggerheads, to break up families with hatred, to blast houses with your deadly flames and your lash. You have a thousand titles, and a thousand ways to do harm. Ransack your heart, that fertile source of ideas, shatter the peace they've arranged, give them reasons for war. Let their warriors ask for, clamour for, arms, then use them at once!'

341–72   Allecto first sets to work on Latinus' wife, who argues about the real meaning of Faunus' oracle.

So Allecto, steeped in the same venom that makes the Gorgons[2] so dangerous, went first of all to Latium and the palace of Latinus. She lay in wait at the quiet entrance of Queen Amata's home; the queen's womanly heart was already seething with grief and anger at the Trojans' arrival, and anxiety for Turnus' marriage. Taking one of the serpents from her blue-black hair Allecto flung it into Amata's breast, where it could worm its way into her heart, so that the queen, crazed by its poison, might shatter her family's peace. Slipping between her dress and the smooth skin of her breasts, gliding unfelt (in her passionate anger the queen didn't notice its movements), it injected her with its own venomous temper. It transformed itself into the coils of her great gold necklace, into the lengths of ribbon that bound her hair, and slithered all over her body.

While the poison was still working its way in with its subtle contagion, beginning to affect her senses and enfold her bones with fire, but before her mind and heart were completely seized by the fever, she spoke gently, as mothers usually do, and in tears at the thought of her daughter marrying a Trojan: 'Father, does Lavinia really have to marry a refugee and a foreigner? Have you no pity for her, or yourself? No feeling for me, her mother? At the first fair wind, that devious pirate will sail off over the seas, taking my daughter with him! Paris sneaked into Sparta, and carried off Helen to Troy – but I suppose you will say that was different! What of your word of honour, of the care you showed in the past for your people? What of the promise you gave so often to Turnus, our nephew? But if our Latin daughter must marry a foreigner – if that is fixed, and the commands of Faunus your father must be obeyed – then, every land that is separate from ours, and not governed by us, to my way of thinking is foreign: *that's* what the oracle means! And Turnus, if we trace back his family tree, comes from Mycenae, in Greece, descended from the first kings of Argos, and they're Grecian too!'

373–94   When Latinus will not listen to her, Amata rushes madly through the city as the poison begins to work, and does what she can herself to thwart the marriage.

All her arguments failed, and she saw that Latinus was adamant. The serpent's mad-making venom sank deep into her heart, and spread right through her; the poor queen, frenzied by grotesque fantasies, raved out of control from end to end of the city, watched by her excitable people . . . Worse was to come: daring a greater crime in the grip of a greater madness, she fled to the woods, and then hid her daughter in mountainside forests, to rob Aeneas of his bride – or at least to delay the wedding. . . The news spread fast; all the rest of the mothers, inflamed by a

114

sympathetic hysteria, were driven by the self-same compulsion to leave their houses and seek a new home, with the open air as a roof . . .

406–34   Allecto next turns her attention to Turnus, urging him to attack the Trojans.

As soon as she felt that the first bout of madness was effective enough, that Latinus' plans and household had been thrown into utter confusion, the baleful Allecto at once flew away on dusky wings to the city of daredevil Turnus. Our ancestors once called the place Ardea; though it still keeps the same great name, its fortunes are now very different. Here in his lofty palace, half-way through the dark night, Turnus lay fast asleep. Allecto cast off the grim looks and shape of a Fury; she changed herself into an old woman, made her face ugly and wrinkled, turned her hair white, and secured it with ribbons and an olive-branch chaplet. So, disguised as Calybe, an ancient priestess from Juno's temple, she appeared to the young man's eyes, and said: 'Turnus, will you let so much hard work go to waste, and your rule be transferred to Trojan settlers? The king is refusing to give you his daughter, or the dowry that was paid for in blood. He's importing a stranger to succeed to the throne. Go on! Make a fool of yourself! Face fresh dangers for him, defeat the Etruscans,[3] bring peace for the Latins – with nothing to show for it! That was the message that almighty Juno told me to bring you, when she came to me while you were sleeping in the peace of night. So, up now! Call out your troops, and march them, gladly, out of the gates to war! Burn up those painted ships with their Trojan captains, who've settled themselves on our beautiful river! The heavenly powers themselves give these orders. If King Latinus won't keep his word and give you his daughter to marry, then let him find out what it's like to have Turnus fighting against him!'

435–74   Turnus ridicules the supposed priestess for what he thinks are her foolish warnings. Allecto angrily retaliates.

But Turnus laughed at the priestess, and began to speak in his turn: 'The news that a fleet has sailed up the Tiber has not, as you think, failed to reach me. Don't dream up such false alarms! Juno has not forgotten us. It is senile decay, madam, dulling your wits and stealing away your sense, that upsets you with needless worries; they are unreal fears that delude you into such warnings. War is for kings. *You* should be worrying about your temple and statues of Juno. Leave peace and war to men; they have to do the fighting!'

His words made Allecto blaze into anger. He was still speaking when his limbs suddenly started to tremble, and his eyes became set and staring. The Fury, with her serpentine hair hissing anger, disclosed her hideous appearance. She fixed him with flaming eyes as he faltered and stammered a few more words. She then thrust him back, as two snakes sprang up on her head like horns. Cracking her whip she spat out her answer in maniacal rage.

'So senile decay dulls my mind, stealing away my sense! I have unreal fears, delusions about wars between kings! Look at me, then! I have come from the home of the Dread Sisters,[4] with war and death in my hand.' With these words she hurled a lance of fire at the prince, thrusting it deep into his chest, where it smouldered with a smoky glow.

He was shaken from his trance by mounting panic, and sweat broke out all over his body, drenching his bones and limbs. Yelling like a madman for weapons, he hunted for sword and shield through his bedroom and palace, seized with a lust for killing and the insane obscenity of war, above all with anger. . . He ordered his army commanders to round up the army and march against King Latinus, who had violated the peace. Italy must be defended, and the enemy thrown out of the country. He could cope with Trojans and Latins together!

After this statement, he called on the gods to witness his vows, while the Rutuli, from a variety of motives, eagerly encouraged each other to fight.

475–537 Allecto next succeeds in turning the Trojans and Latin people against each other.

While Turnus was inspiring his people with daredevil courage,

Allecto whirled on Stygian wings to the Trojans, with a fresh scheme in mind: she had spotted the place where the handsome Iulus was hunting along the shore with his dogs and snares. Hellish Allecto suddenly sent his hounds mad, tickled their nostrils with a well-known scent to send them streaming after a stag in full cry. This was the beginning of trouble, for it put the spark of war in the hearts of the countryfolk.

There was a stag, a splendid animal with a fine spread of antlers. It had been taken away from its mother when young, and reared as a pet by Tyrrhus and his children. He was the royal huntsman, and looked after the herds of deer and the broad hunting-grounds. The boys' sister, Silvia, had patiently taught it to obey her, and woven chains of wild flowers for its antlers. She combed the beast's coat, and washed it in fresh spring water. It put up with the children's handling, and came to Tyrrhus' table. It ran wild in the woods, but at night, no matter how late it was, would make for home by itself, and find its way to the stable.

It was roaming far from home, floating down the river, or seeking relief from the heat in the shade of the trees on the bank, when Iulus' maddened hounds sent it scuttling in panic. Iulus himself was desperately keen on such a fine trophy, bent back his bow and shot. The Fury must have guided his uncertain aim, and the arrow hummed wickedly through the animal's flanks and belly. Wounded, it dragged itself home for safety, and, whimpering, found its stable. The bloodstained creature filled the whole house with its almost human cries. Silvia first, flailing her arms in despair, shouted for help, and called out her tough countrymen. They arrived with surprising speed – for ruthless Allecto was lurking in the silent woods – armed with sharp sticks baked hard in the fire, or large knotty fence-posts, so angry that whatever they grabbed would do to fight with.

Tyrrhus, it happened, had been splitting oak logs with wedges. He snatched up an axe, arrived panting with anger, and mustered his men. From her watchpoint the fierce Fury saw that this was her chance to make havoc. She flew to the steep roof of the stables and from its high ridge sounded the shepherds' alarm-call on a bugle, with a blast from hell. The woods and deep forests trembled and echoed at the note. Then, at the call on that sinister horn, snatching up weapons, work-hardened farm-hands came running from every direction. The Trojan warriors, too, poured from the gates of the camp to help Iulus. They drew up in lines of battle – this was no rustic brawl fought out with stout clubs or fire-hardened cudgels: now two-edged steel would decide. On both sides a grim crop of drawn swords bristled; bronze armour gleamed in the sunlight's challenge, reflecting the rays to the sky. So too, at sea, white horses appear when the wind starts to blow; then the sea gradually heaves up high, and the waves get steeper, till from the depths of the troughs they mount to the sky.

Now Tyrrhus' eldest son, Almo, in the front rank was laid low by a whirring arrow. The wound was deep in his throat, choking the path of his liquid voice and his fragile life with blood. There were bodies all round him, including old Galaesus, one of the finest and richest men in Italy, who had run between the lines to try to make peace.

540–8   Allecto reports to Juno.

While the battle, still equally balanced, raged over the plains, now that Allecto had fulfilled her promise by giving the war its baptism of blood with the deaths in the first minutes of fighting, she flew out of Italy, wheeling up to the air of heaven. In triumph she proudly reported to Juno: 'There, I've arranged your discord for you, and bitter hostility! Try telling them now to be friends, or to make an alliance, now that I've splashed the Trojans with Italian blood!'

549–71   Juno, aware that to do more would arouse Jupiter's anger, refuses Allecto's offer to spread the war more widely in Italy. Allecto returns to hell.

572–804   The Latins carry their dead and wounded back into their city. Impelled by Turnus' anger, and the excitement aroused by Amata, they call on Latinus to declare war. He cannot dissuade them, and withdraws from public life into his palace. When the people demand that, in accordance with ancient custom, he should open the Gates of War in the temple of Janus, he refuses, so Juno herself breaks them open. Preparations for war are made throughout Latium. Then there follows a list of twelve Italian tribes and their leaders who have gathered to help expel the Trojans from their country, culminating in Turnus and his Rutuli. The thirteenth leader is very different.

In addition to these, from the Volscian nation, at the head of a squadron of cavalry in dazzling bronze armour, came the warrior princess Camilla. Her feminine hands were not used to baskets of wool and the spinning wheel. She was tough enough, although a girl, to face battle, and outrun the winds. You could imagine her racing over the blades of standing corn without bruising the tender ears as she ran, or skimming lightly above the waves of the swelling sea without wetting the speeding soles of her feet. Youngsters and housewives came crowding from field and cottage to gaze in awe as she passed. They gaped in wonder at the royal purple, how gracefully it cloaked her smooth shoulders, and at the golden clasp in her hair, at the Lycian quiver she wore and the steel-tipped myrtle-wood shepherd's staff that served as her spear.

Notes to Book VII

1   **Scylla**   A monster which seized and devoured mariners that sailed near its cave, which overlooked the straits between Italy and Sicily, with the whirlpool of Charybdis opposite the cave. Juno had failed to wreck Aeneas' fleet on the African sandbanks on its storm-driven flight to Libya.

2   **Gorgons**   The three Gorgons were horrifying monsters whose hideous heads had snakes for hair. Anything which met the gaze of the head was turned to stone.

3   **Etruscans**   A people living north of Latium. Virgil refers to a legend that Turnus was helping Latinus in a war against the Etruscans.

4   **the Dread Sisters**   The Furies.

Book VIII

Turnus, while collecting forces to fight the Trojans, sends to ask for the help of Diomede, a Greek warrior who had settled in Italy after the sack of Troy.

Aeneas is told in a dream by the river-god Tiberinus to make an alliance with King Evander, living up river in the small settlement of Pallanteum, on the future site of Rome. The next night the current is magically stilled, and Aeneas sails. He is welcomed by Evander, who explains that they are in the middle of a festival in honour of Hercules. Hercules had killed a giant named Cacus, who, from his cave on the Aventine hill, had been terrorising the neighbourhood. In the evening Evander tells Aeneas of the early history of Latium, of the so-called Golden Age under Saturn, and takes him on a tour of the city, explaining the origin of various Roman sites and names.

Meanwhile on Olympus Venus, alarmed by all the anti-Trojan activity in Italy, persuades her husband Vulcan to make magic armour for her son. At the same time, in Italy, Evander promises Aeneas his help. He advises him to seek an alliance with the Etruscans and their leader, Tarchon. Aeneas, he says, will be warmly welcomed by the Etruscans, for their previous king, Mezentius, banished for his appalling cruelty, was now being helped by Turnus in a war against them. Moreover the Etruscans had been warned by an oracle that only a foreigner could lead them to success in this war.

When Aeneas sees a miraculous sign in the sky he agrees to go, and sets out with Evander's son Pallas. On entering the Etruscan camp he is met by Venus, who gives him the armour. The shield is covered in engraved scenes from Roman history, and this is described in detail. In this way Virgil is again able to link the distant legendary past with his own times, and to make the triumphs of the emperor Augustus appear almost destined by fate.

Characters

Aeneas
Evander, king of the small settlement of Pallanteum
Pallas, his son
Mezentius, former king of the Etruscans, who dwelt in Italy
    north of the river Tiber; he had been banished for his
    cruelty

310–36   After the festival in honour of Hercules has been
concluded, Evander takes his guests round his humble city of
Pallanteum, the future site of Rome.

Aeneas was gazing with ready admiration at everything around
him: he was charmed by the place, and eagerly asked for details
of the heroic days of the past, and listened to the stories behind
them. Then King Evander, founder of Rome's citadel, went on to
say: 'These groves were the homes of the nymphs and fauns that
were born here, and of a race of men who sprang from tough
oak-tree trunks. They had no laws or culture; they knew nothing
of ploughing, of storing food, or rationing out their store, but
lived off the fruit of trees and what the rigours of hunting
provided. Saturn was the first to arrive; he was an exile, deprived
of his kingdom and in flight from the heights of Olympus and
Jupiter's might. He united these ignorant peoples, scattered over
the hills, and gave them laws. He chose to call the place Latium,
because he had been able to hide[1] here safely. The Golden Age is
the name men give to the time when he ruled, for his subjects
enjoyed settled peace. Then, little by little, the times grew worse,
and gold gave way to a dimmer and different metal, with mad
war-fever and love of material possessions.

'Then there arrived a mob of invaders from further inland,
and Latium changed its name more than once. Then there were
tyrants, like Thybris, a huge uncivilised fellow; from him, some
time later, we Italians called our river the Tiber, replacing its old
name of Albula. I was the next to settle here, driven from my
homeland by all-powerful Fortune and inescapable Fate, in search
of the end of the sea. It was the dread warning of my mother,[2] the
nymph Carmentis, and Apollo's instructions, that brought me.'

337–58   Evander moves on to point out various sites that were to
become famous in later times, until they reach his own home.

359–69   With such talk as this they came to the house of
humble Evander. Everywhere cattle were lowing, in what is now
the Forum, and the rich suburb overlooking it. When they'd sat
down, he said: 'After he'd beaten Cacus, Hercules came in here,

121

this house was big enough for him. So, my friend, have the courage to despise possessions; make yourself, like him, worthy of becoming a god, don't be scornful of poverty.' Then he led the great frame of Aeneas beneath the roof of his humble dwelling, and showed him to a bed with a mattress of leaves and the skin of a Libyan bear to cover them. Night came flying, folding the earth in her dusky wings.

370–422   That same night, as they lay in bed, Venus beguiled her husband Vulcan into making some armour for her son. Waking early, he goes to his forge in one of the Lipari Islands.

423–53   Virgil describes Vulcan's orders and the activities of his workmen.

Here then the Fire-God came, descending from heaven above. In a huge cave the Cyclopes were working iron: Brontes, Steropes and Pyracmon,[3] stripped naked. They had in their hands the cast of a thunderbolt, the sort which Jupiter hurls to the earth in hundreds from all over heaven. Part had been polished, but the rest was unfinished. They had given it three rays of driving rain, three more of rain-cloud, three of red fire, and three of the winged south wind. Now they were adding the terrifying flashes, the noise and the panic, the anger in the following flames.

Elsewhere they were working on a swift-wheeled chariot for Mars, in which he rouses both men and cities to war. Others were busily polishing the fearful aegis[4] that Athena wears when she's angry, rubbing the scaly gold snake-skin, the intertwined serpents, the Gorgon-head[5] (the centre-piece, on the breast of the goddess), a severed head rolling its eyes.

'Stop everything, Cyclopes of Etna, put aside the jobs you've started! Turn your attention to this; we've got to make arms for a red-blooded hero! This is when you need strength, busy hands, your very best craftsmanship! Get cracking!'

He did not have to say another word; quickly they all set to work, sharing the jobs between them. Molten bronze and gold flowed in streams, and wound-dealing steel was melted in an enormous furnace. They shaped out a massive shield, enough by itself to withstand everything the Latins might throw at it, welding seven round layers of metal together. Some of the

Cyclopes worked away at the bellows, pumping gales of air in and out, others tempered hissing bronze in water. The cave groaned under the weight of their anvils, as rhythmic blows fell on them, delivered by powerful arms, as they kept the lumps of iron turning in strong-jawed tongs.

454–69   Meanwhile, in Italy, Evander goes with his son Pallas to greet Aeneas and Achates.

470–517   Evander advises Aeneas to seek an alliance with the Etruscans. He explains why he thinks Aeneas' approach will be welcomed.

'Great Trojan general, while you are alive I will never admit that Troy, or its hopes of success, are defeated. But our insignificant strength cannot match your great reputation, for on one side we're shut in by the Tiber, on the other the Rutuli threaten us, clashing their arms round our walls. But I intend to make you the ally of mighty peoples with fortified cities and a wealth of power, a way to safety unexpectedly offered by chance. It is the hand of Fate that guided you here.

'Not far away lies the city of Caere, founded on ancient rock. A famous warlike people, the Lydians, long ago settled on that Etruscan hill. For a long time they flourished, till King Mezentius, with tyrannical power and ruthless forces, oppressed them. I will not recall the unspeakable murders and bestial crimes he committed. May the gods save up the same sort of thing for him, and his family! He even tied living men to corpses, binding them hand to hand, and mouth to mouth, a form of torture in which they died a lingering death, dripping with diseased and putrefied matter in that sickening embrace.

'At last his people tired of oppression, took up arms and besieged the monstrous lunatic in his own palace, cut down his henchmen and threw firebrands on to the roof. However, he escaped in the carnage, and fled to the Rutuli, and asked Turnus, a friend of the family, for protection. So all the Etruscans have risen, quite rightly, in fury, mustered their army and demanded their king back to face his punishment, with the threat of immediate war if they don't get him.

'There are thousands of them, Aeneas, and I will make you

their leader. Their troop-ships are thick on the shore, grumbling and demanding invasion, but an aged sooth-sayer is delaying them by revealing the fates: "You men are the best troops in all 'Etruria, fine examples of the courage and honour of our ancient race. Mezentius deserves your hatred; the anger that drives you against him is justified. But no Italian may command your splendid army, it's forbidden by Fate; you must find a commander from overseas." So the Etruscan army, alarmed by this warning, has settled down on the plain there. Tarchon himself sent ambassadors to me with the royal crown and sceptre, and offered the badges of general, if I would go to their camp, and take over the Etruscan command. But old age is upon me, cold and slow, and I'm worn out by the passage of time; it warns me to refuse the command – I'm no longer fit for adventures.

'I would encourage my son to go, but the blood from his Sabine mother[6] makes him half-Italian. But Fate approves of *your* age and descent, it is you the gods have chosen. So set out on your task, most gallant leader of Trojans, and now of Italians too. What's more, though he is my hope and comfort, I'll send Pallas with you. Let him learn from your teaching how to endure war service and the burden of war itself. Let him watch what you do and model himself on you, right from these early days of his youth.'

518–616 From a clear sky there is a sudden crash of thunder. They look up to see the magical weapons in the sky. Aeneas tells them that Venus promised to send such a sign if war threatened, and that victory over his enemies is certain. He sends messengers back to the camp by the shore to tell Ascanius of his mission to Caere. Evander bids Pallas a tearful farewell, begging to be allowed to die himself before he hears news of his son's death. Aeneas and Pallas set out; later in the day and weary from their journey, they are resting when Venus appears and presents Aeneas with the magic arms.

617–41 Aeneas examines the weapons. The shield is round. A circular central section is engraved with pictures of Augustus' final battle and triumph over his enemies. A gold band separates this part from eight scenes of earlier Roman history in an outer circle. Virgil has chosen subjects which would in themselves make good pictures: but they also show events and people that

are typical of the steadfast qualities which made Rome
Virgil is thus letting Aeneas see the future for which he
(The events are explained in the notes on pp. 128

Aeneas could not stop gazing at the arms that Venus had
given him, overjoyed with the honour she had done him, and
scrutinised each in turn. In admiration he turned in his hands
the helmet, with its menacing plumes (it seemed to be flashing
fire), the death-dealing sword, and the breastplate of reinforced
bronze, blood-red and huge like a dark cloud lit to a glow by the
rays of the sun, and gleaming afar. Then he picked up the
polished shin-guards with inlays of gold and electrum, the spear,
and the fabulously crafted shield.

On the shield the Fire-God had engraved events of Italian
history and Roman successes, for being acquainted with
prophets he was well aware of the future. Upon it appeared the
whole line to be born of Ascanius, and in succession the wars
that they fought. He had pictured a mother-wolf[7] lying in the
green cave of Mars, while the twin boys played and tugged at her
teats, unafraid as they sucked her milk. She had bent back her
shapely neck, nuzzling each one in turn, and licking them into
shape.

Next, he had depicted Rome, when the Sabine women[8] were
lawlessly snatched from the audience round the arena during the
Great Circus Games, and the sudden start of the new war which
Romulus' people fought with old Tatius and his stern Sabines.
Later the same kings ended their quarrel,[9] and stood in full
armour by Jupiter's altar, each holding a chalice and sacrificing
a sow to ratify their treaty.

642–70   Other features and events of Roman history, down to
Virgil's own times, are described.

In the next picture, two chariots had been driven apart to tear
Mettus of Alba[10] to pieces – you shouldn't have broken your
word, Mettus! Tullus was dragging bits of the liar's body
through a wood, splashing the bushes and dyeing them red with
his blood.

Porsenna[11] was there, telling the Romans to take back the
Tarquin whom they had banished, gripping the city tight in a

125

ᴌighty seige, while Aeneas' descendants rushed to the sword in defence of their liberty. He actually looked, in the picture, just like a real person yelling indignant threats, because Horatius was daring to break down the bridge, and Cloelia had slipped out of her bonds and was swimming across the river.

At the top of the shield Manlius,[12] guardian of the Tarpeian rock, stood in front of the temple, protecting the Capitol, where Romulus' palace looked rough with its newly thatched roof. Here, too, a goose, in silver, flew through the golden porticoes, squawking a warning that the Gauls were near. And the Gauls were there, under cover of the darkness that the luck of a cloudy night had given them, creeping through the bushes up to the citadel. Their clothing and hair were in gold. They gleamed in their short striped cloaks, with necklets of gold round their milk-white necks. Each of them brandished a pair of Alpine pikes in his hand, protecting himself with an oblong shield.

Next, the Fire-God had worked in relief scenes of religious significance – the priests of Mars dancing, the priests of Pan naked, wearing their wool-tufted helmets; the sacred shield[13] dropped from the sky by the gods; virtuous ladies taking the sacred vessels in procession through the city in soft-cushioned carriages. By them he had pictured the huge gates of Tartarus and the torments of the damned,[14] like Catiline hanging from a towering cliff, and quaking at the sight of the Furies' faces. Good people, in the care of Cato, were in the adjoining section.

Inside these scenes ran a band of gold representing the wide swelling ocean, the dark water flecked with white spray. All round the circle dolphins, picked out in silver, cut through the water, lashing the surface with their tails.

671–731   The centre of the shield shows four aspects of Augustus' victory[15] over Antony and Cleopatra in the battle of Actium.

In the centre could be seen two fleets in bronze, fighting the battle of Actium. You could see the fever of activity round Cape Leucate where it took place – the sea here was a bright gleam of gold. On one side Augustus Caesar, high on the stern, was leading the Italians to battle, the people and senate behind him, with the gods of the home and the state. Twin flames flashed from his forehead, triumphant, while the star of his father rose over him. His lieutenant Agrippa, with the gods and winds in his favour, proudly led out his column of ships; on his head, his proud war-decoration, shone the naval crown, with its distinctive figure-heads.

On the other side in barbaric splendour, with an assortment of equipment, sailed Antony,[16] fresh from his victories on the shore of the Indian Ocean. In his fleet was the might of Egypt, the Far East, and also, disgracefully, his Egyptian wife Cleopatra. As the fleets came dashing together the whole sea was churned into foam by the three-pronged bows and the strokes of the oars. As they headed out to the deep you'd have thought that islands, torn up by their roots, were afloat, that mountains were buffeting mountains, to see those high-towered ships which their crews sailed out to war. Fire-darts, with burning flax tied to them, flew thick and fast, and the sea turned red from this fresh slaughter.

In the middle Queen Cleopatra[17] was arousing her fleet with Egyptian cymbals, unable as yet to see the two snakes of death behind her. Monstrous gods in all shapes and sizes, like barking dog-headed Anubis, had taken up arms against Neptune, Minerva and Venus. Engraved in iron was Mars, raging in the thick of the fighting. Grim Furies hovered over the battle; Discord, her clothes in tatters, joined in exultantly; and the Goddess of War flailed her bloodstained whip in the rear.

At the sight of all this Apollo[18] was pointing his bow down at them from his temple at Actium; in panic the Egyptians, Indians and Arabs all turned and fled. Cleopatra herself could be seen, as she prayed for a fair wind, spreading sail, anxiously paying out the ropes. The Fire-God had shown her, pale at the coming of death in the midst of the carnage, swept on by the westerly winds and waves. Facing her, he had put the great river-god Nile, mourning and opening the folds of his cloak, with a sweep of his robes inviting the conquered into the bosom of his dark waters, the hiding-place of his streams.

Augustus[19] rode in through the walls of Rome to triumph for his three victories; he was dedicating three hundred great shrines all over the city – the immortal offering he had sworn to the gods of Italy. The streets rang with applause, rejoicing and revelry. In every temple choirs of women were singing and the altars were blazing; the ground by the altars was covered with the bodies of sacrificed bullocks.

In the snow-white porch of Apollo's dazzling temple[20] the

emperor himself was surveying the gifts from his various peoples, displaying them on the proud temple-gates. Conquered tribes filed past in an endless procession – languages, clothes and weapons in endless variety. There were Nomads,[21] and Africans with loose flowing robes; Carians from Asia Minor and bowmen from the Ukraine; a tableau of the Euphrates, less troubled now; from the ends of the earth the Morini from Belgium were there, the Rhine with its two mouths; untamable Scythians and the Armenian river Araxes resenting its bridge.

Such were the scenes Aeneas admired on the shield that Vulcan had made and Venus had given him. Though he knew nothing about these events, he rejoiced in the pictures of them, as he raised on his shoulder the fame and fortune of his children's children.

Notes to Book VIII

1 **to hide** The Latin word for 'to hide' is *latere*, and Evander believes that this accounts for the name Latium.

2 **the dread warning of my mother** Evander had committed some crime: it is not known what he had done.

3 **Brontes, Steropes and Pyracmon** Their names mean 'Thunderer', 'Lightning' and 'Fire-anvil': they worked in a cave underneath the volcano Etna.

4 **aegis** This was a divine shield carried by Jupiter and Athena; here it is thought of as a breastplate, with a Gorgon's head at the centre.

5 **Gorgon-head** The Gorgons were hideous monsters with hair formed of serpents, whose gaze turned anyone to stone.

6 **Sabine mother** The Sabines were an ancient people living in Italy next to the Latins.

7 **mother-wolf** *(Scene 1)* Romulus and Remus were the sons of Rhea Silvia, daughter of the last king of Alba Longa. Their father was said to be Mars. Their uncle threw them into the Tiber, but they were washed ashore and suckled by a she-wolf, which became the most famous of Rome's pictorial emblems.

8 **the Sabine women** *(Scene 2)* When Romulus had built his new city, he secured wives for his people by inviting the neighbouring Sabines to a festival in the Circus, and then carrying off the Sabine womenfolk.

9 **ended their quarrel** *(Scene 3)* The war between the Sabines, led by their king Tatius, and the Romans was brought to an end by the captured women. The two tribes then united.

10 **Mettus of Alba** *(Scene 4)* Mettus, who became the dictator of Alba Longa, broke his treaty with Rome. As a punishment he was tied to two chariots which were driven in different directions and tore his body apart. Tullus was king of Rome.

11 **Porsenna** *(Scene 5)* King of the Etruscans *c.* 510 BC; he besieged Rome, trying to restore Tarquin the banished king of Rome to his throne.

Horatius Cocles defended a bridge over the Tiber while it was being broken down behind him. Cloelia was a Roman girl given to Porsenna as a hostage, but she escaped and swam across the river to safety.

12 **Manlius** *(Scene 6)* The Gauls occupied Rome *c.* 390 BC. The sacred geese warned the Roman general Manlius that the Gauls were trying to storm the Capitol.

13 **the sacred shield** *(Scene 7)* A shield was said to have fallen from heaven as a sign of the gods' good will towards Rome. King Numa had eleven copies of it made to prevent it being stolen, and these were looked after by the Salii, the priests of Mars. The priests of Pan, or Faunus, were called the Luperci. Roman matrons were allowed to ride in upholstered carriages when taking part in religious ceremonies.

14 **torments of the damned** *(Scene 8)* Catiline is shown being punished in Tartarus for leading an attempt to overthrow the state in 63 BC. Cato is an example of just and virtuous statesmanship, even though he committed suicide in 46 BC to avoid falling into the hands of Julius Caesar: he dwells in Elysium, the part of the Underworld reserved for successful and happy men.

15 **Augustus' victory** Augustus was the grandson of Julius Caesar's sister, and was chosen as Caesar's heir. He became the first emperor of Rome after defeating his enemies, Antony and Cleopatra, in a naval battle off Cape Actium in Greece in 31 BC. Agrippa was his second-in-command, and responsible for most of Augustus' victories in the long war: he had won the 'naval crown' in 36 BC. At Actium he commanded Augustus' 400 vessels against the 230 of Antony and the 60 of Cleopatra.

16 **Antony** Mark Antony had been married to Augustus' sister Octavia, but fell in love with Queen Cleopatra, and tried to take over the eastern half of the Roman empire – hence the reference to victories in the Indian Ocean.

17 **Queen Cleopatra** She is depicted as a dangerous foreigner aided by monstrous foreign gods. Their battle with the great Roman gods is the second of the four central scenes.

18 **Apollo** In the third central scene Cleopatra is shown in flight from the battle of Actium with her fleet. Virgil suggests that Apollo, whose temple overlooked the battle, was responsible.

19 **Augustus** The last scene, in two parts, shows the triple triumph of Augustus on 13, 14 and 15 August 29 BC, in which he rode into the city on a chariot pulled by four white horses to celebrate his victories in Illyricum, at Actium and in Egypt.

20 **Apollo's dazzling temple** In the second part of the last scene Augustus sits by the white marble temple to Apollo on the Palatine hill, which was dedicated in 28 BC.

21 **Nomads** The exotic names of the remote peoples conquered by the Romans were always of great interest to Roman poets and historians.

Book IX

Juno sends Iris to tell Turnus to attack the Trojans while Aeneas is away, and he blockades the Trojan camp. When the Trojans stay resolutely inside their ramparts, as instructed by Aeneas before his departure, Turnus sets their ships on fire. But the ships are magically turned into beautiful sea-nymphs which swim safely away.

Nisus, one of the competitors in the foot race in Book V, now sees that the Italians are becoming careless, and makes plans to slide through the blockade, to take news of it to Aeneas. Euryalus insists on joining him, and on their way out they stumble on some of the enemy, lying in a drunken stupor, and slaughter them. However, they are seen by an enemy cavalry unit, pursued and killed.

On the following day the Italians again assault the Trojan ramparts, with the heads of Nisus and Euryalus displayed on spears. There are many casualties on both sides, and Ascanius wins praise for killing his first man. Turnus gets into the Trojan camp when the gates are briefly opened for an abortive raid. He could have opened the gates again to let his troops in, but instead, in a desire for personal triumph, he presses on alone, killing many Trojans, till he is forced to escape by diving into the Tiber.

❦❦❦❦❦

It is in this book that fighting becomes the major topic. Epic poems – great narrative stories like Homer's *Iliad* and *Odyssey* – are properly concerned with deeds of heroic prowess, death and bloodshed. Yet Virgil's attitude to war was quite different from Homer's. Virgil's personal hatred for the violence and brutality of war is obvious in his earlier poems. This conflict between his personal feelings and the subject matter of this second half of the *Aeneid* is clearly visible in this Book. In particular it can be seen in this episode, when stark descriptions of the horrors of war (like the slaughter of the sleeping Rutuli by Nisus and Euryalus, and the deaths of the two friends) are combined with intensely felt pity for its victims. Virgil's distaste for this sort of topic is also perhaps the cause of the very incongruity of the fairy-tale story of Aeneas' ships turned into sea-nymphs interrupting accounts of grim fighting.

Characters

Trojans
Nisus and Euryalus
Mnestheus, Serestus

Italians
Rhamnes and Messapus, killed while asleep by Nisus and
Euryalus
Volcens, Sulmo, Tagus

 1–167   The Italians have made an unsuccessful attack on the
Trojan camp and ships. They make preparations for another
attack on the following day.

168–223   Nisus and Euryalus plan a daring deed to alert
Aeneas.

The Trojans too were equipped and ready, and from their
vantage-point on the rampart looked down on these preparations. In some anxiety they urgently tested the gates, and with
sword in hand they went on making ways up to the defence
towers. Mnestheus and forceful Serestus took the lead, for
Aeneas had ordered that they should have the command if ever a
crisis required it. The whole force was now deployed on the
walls: they had drawn lots for the places of danger, and now took
their turns on guard at the posts assigned to them.
   The sentry at one gate was Nisus, a most stalwart fighter, and
a fine shot with spear or arrow. Beside him stood his friend
Euryalus – no handsomer warrior had ever put on Trojan
armour, a youngster whose unshaven cheeks were showing the
first signs of manhood. They were in love, and charged into
battle together; now too they shared sentry duty. Nisus said:
'Euryalus, do the gods put the longing for action into our minds,
or do we make the gods an excuse for our own aggressiveness?
For a long time I've been itching to dash into battle, or to do
something big; I'm tired of this peace and quiet. You see how
confident the Rutuli are! They have only a few watch-fires
burning. They lie there, flat out in a drunken sleep; the whole
camp is silent. Listen to a scheme I'm debating, an idea that's
jumped into my head.

131

'All our leaders and people are demanding that Aeneas be called back, that men should be sent to report what has happened. I shall ask a reward for going, and if they promise to give it to you – for myself the glory of doing it is all I want – I think I can find a way, past the foot of that hill, to the ramparts and walls of Pallanteum.'

Euryalus was stunned, then, overcome by a pressing desire for glory himself, he spoke at once to his eager friend: 'Nisus! Don't you want to take me with you on such an adventure? Do you think I would let you face such enormous risks on your own? That's not how my gallant father taught me to behave, as he brought me up in the Greek reign of terror and the ordeals of Troy. I've never treated you like that since I joined up with great-hearted Aeneas, wherever our destiny took us. I am really not so fond of my life that I wouldn't be glad to lose it for the honour you're seeking.'

Nisus replied: 'I never feared anything like that from you, believe me! I couldn't, it wouldn't be right! I pray that great Jupiter – or whoever it is that rewards us as we deserve – may bring me triumphantly back to you. But if some accident or some god should sink the attempt – you often see things go wrong in such risky affairs – I shouldn't like you to die. You are young, and deserve more of life. Let there be someone to hurry my body away from the battlefield, or ransom it, and then give it burial. And if Fortune should somehow deny it a grave, let someone perform the death rites, and give it the honour of a cenotaph. Nor could I bear to cause your mother such grief: she was the only mother who dared to follow her son[1] and leave Acestes' city behind.'

But Euryalus answered: 'It's no use inventing excuses! My mind is made up and nothing will change it. Let's get on with it!' He woke up the guards, who took over and kept up the watch. The pair of them left their post and went to look for Ascanius.

224–353 They find the Trojan leaders in a midnight conference, discussing what to do, and whom to send to Aeneas. When Nisus explains how they intend to break through the blockade, their enterprise is greeted with admiration and joy. Ascanius promises lavish rewards if they can bring Aeneas back, and undertakes to look after Euryalus' mother, whatever may happen. As they creep through the enemy lines they stumble upon bodies lying in drunken sleep. First Nisus, then Euryalus, start killing them brutally as they lie there.

354–445   They soon regret this delay.

Nisus realised that Euryalus was being carried too far by his lust for blood. 'We must stop now,' he called, 'the dawn is near, and light means danger for us. That's vengeance enough, we've cleared a path through the enemy!'

They left untouched numerous solid silver weapons and wine-bowls as well as some beautiful coverlets. But the decorations Rhamnes had worn on his breastplate, and his gold-studded sword-belt, these Euryalus seized and slung over his own strong shoulders – though he had little joy of them. Then he put on his own head the well-made helmet of Messapus with its bright plumes. They left the camp then, and headed for safety.

Meanwhile some cavalry, sent out while the rest of the Italian army remained deployed on the plain, were coming in from Latinus' city with despatches for Turnus. There were three hundred of them, fully equipped, under the command of Volcens. They were getting close to the camp and approaching the walls when, in the distance, they caught sight of the two Trojans, turning away to the left. It was his helmet that betrayed Euryalus – he had forgotten about it – reflecting the moonbeams in the shadowy half-light of night. There was no mistaking what it meant. Volcens called from the column: 'Halt, you men! Who are you, armed like that? Where are you going? What are you doing here?'

Without reply they ran hard for the woods, trusting the darkness to save them.

But the horsemen, knowing the side roads, galloped left and right to block their escape, and encircled the wood to guard every exit. The wood was a tangle throughout of briars and dark-green holm-oaks, completely choked with brambles – only a track here or there could be glimpsed in the barely-seen clearings. In the gloom Euryalus was hampered by the branches and the weight of his booty, and fear made him mistake his direction. Nisus had got clean away; without thinking of anything else he had slipped right past the enemy, when he stopped, and looked round for his friend – in vain. He was missing.

'Euryalus, my poor friend, where did I lose you? Where shall I look?' At once he retraced all the twists and turns of his route through the maze of the wood, carefully tracking his footsteps back, and slipped through the silent bushes. Then he heard horses, and the noise that signalled pursuit. Hardly a moment passed before a loud cry came to his ears, and he caught sight of Euryalus. He had been perplexed by the treacherous wood and the darkness, and the sudden bewildering uproar: a whole gang of the enemy caught him, dragging him off despite all his futile struggles.

What was Nisus to do? Was there some daring or violent move that would rescue his friend? Or should he hurl himself to a certain death on their swords, a quick and glorious end from his wounds? Swiftly he drew back his spear arm, looking up to the moon above, and prayed: 'O goddess, come to my aid in this plight, you who are goddess of hunting[2] and queen of the stars and woods: if ever my father on my behalf brought gifts to your altars, if ever I brought you gifts of my own that I had won in the chase to hang in your sacred temple, grant that I may rout this gang, and guide my spear through the air!' Then with every ounce of his strength he threw. The flying spear split the darkness of night and struck into Sulmo's back. It snapped off short, but the splintered shaft still passed through his heart. A warm stream of blood gushed from his chest and as long gasping sobs racked his side he dropped to the ground, and grew cold.

His companions looked all around them. Nisus, now even fiercer, launched another spear from up by his ear. Pandemonium reigned as it went whizzing in one side of Tagus' head and out of the other, and, warmed by his blood, stuck fast, right through his brain. Volcens was raging with anger, but couldn't see where the weapon had come from, or where to make his furious counter-attack. 'Well then!' he cried, 'in the mean time you shall pay for both of their lives with your own life-blood!' Drawing his sword he went for Euryalus.

Then Nisus was terrified out of his senses and yelled: he could no longer hide in the darkness and endure such a burden of grief. 'Here! Look! I am the one who did it! Turn your swords on me! It was all my fault; he wouldn't and couldn't have done it! I swear by heaven and the all-seeing stars. His only fault was loving his unlucky friend too well!'

Those were Nisus' words, but by then the sword had been violently driven and thrust through the younger man's ribs, laying his white chest open. Euryalus shuddered, and died.

Blood ran over his beautiful body, and his head, top-heavy, sank down on his shoulders. In the same way a scarlet flower, when its roots are slashed by the ploughshare, sags and dies, or poppy-heads droop on weary stems, weighed down by rain-drops.

Nisus hurled himself full at them, making for Volcens, intent only on Volcens. The enemy crowded close around him on this side and that, to force him away. But nothing could stop him, till, whirling his sword like a thunderbolt, he buried it deep in Volcens' screaming face and, dying himself, killed his enemy. Then, pierced through and through with wounds, he fell on his lifeless friend's body, and at last found peace in the calm of death.

Notes to Book IX

1 **dared to follow her son** He is referring to the incident in Book V when many of the women and faint-hearted Trojans stayed behind in Sicily.
2 **goddess of hunting** Diana has three forms: in the sky she is the moon, on earth the goddess of hunting, beneath the earth Hecate, queen of ghosts.

Book X

This book opens with a council of the gods. Jupiter is indignant that fighting between Trojans and Italians still continues, and forbids any more intervention in the war by the gods. An angry argument follows between Venus and Juno about the part each has taken in supporting her favourites. Jupiter will not take sides, and says that he will leave Fate to decide what will happen: any man's future will be decided by his own actions. (Most of the remainder of the book is then taken up by scenes of battle in which the characters do indeed decide their own fate.)

The siege of the Trojan camp continues, and Aeneas returns from his mission in search of Etruscan help with a large Etruscan contingent, led by Tarchon. Fighting begins again, without either side gaining the upper hand. Evander's son Pallas insists on meeting Turnus in single combat and is killed. Turnus behaves with cruel arrogance, and strips Pallas' body of its distinctive sword-belt. Aeneas, enraged by the news, storms over the battlefield causing havoc among the Italians. Awed by his power Juno, with Jupiter's permission, extricates Turnus from the battle. Leadership of the Italian forces is then taken by Mezentius, the banished Etruscan king, till he meets Aeneas in battle. When Mezentius is wounded, his son, Lausus, intervenes to save him, but is killed by Aeneas. Aeneas, unlike Turnus, is affected by deep sorrow at what he has to do, and restores Lausus' body to his comrades. Mezentius, on hearing of his son's death, rides out to face Aeneas again, and meets a heroic and dignified end.

❦ ❦ ❦

Book X is dominated by the three duels. Virgil's account of the deaths of Pallas and Lausus emphasises the futiliti of the deaths in battle of the same young men who might have done most to benefit their fellow men. It also demonstrates the difference between Aeneas and Turnus. First, Turnus is arrogantly confident that he can kill Pallas, and he does so with the typical martial efficiency of an epic hero. The news sends Aeneas on a wave of killing, as savage as any action of Turnus. Then he despatches Lausus with ruthless brutality. But suddenly Aeneas is overcome with revulsion for the cruelty of war, and he treats the dying Lausus with pity and sympathy; unlike Turnus he displays those qualities that do give some hope for human progress.

Mezentius' death, however, is deserved, and a true reason for the subjects of Mezentius to rejoice; yet even here Virgil arouses some pathos, and even admiration for the courage of Mezentius as he dies.

Characters

Gods
Jupiter

Trojans and allies
Aeneas
Tarchon, leader of the Etruscans
Pallas, son of Evander

Italians
Turnus
Mezentius, the banished Etruscan king
Lausus, his son

 1–99   Jupiter has summoned the gods and warned them not to interfere in the war. Venus complains bitterly about Juno's interventions. Juno with equal vehemence denies causing any of the Trojans' disasters, but says that any help she may give give to Troy's enemies is justified.

100–17   Jupiter states his own position – he will leave everything to the Fates.

Then the almighty Father, master of the universe, began to speak. At his first word the high home of the gods fell silent, the earth shook to its foundations and the heavens were still; the winds stopped blowing and the surface of the sea grew calm.

'Lock these words in your hearts, and never forget them. The Italians and Trojans have been prevented from coming to some understanding, and you two will not make an end of your differences. Whatever luck any man has today, whatever they hope to achieve – Trojan or Italian – I will not treat them differently. Aeneas' camp may be blockaded today because that is the Italian's destiny, or because they have made a dreadful mistake, or taken misguided advice. This applies to the Italians,

137

too. Each man's efforts will decide the fortune he'll get, good or bad. I am Jupiter, king, and completely impartial. The Fates will take their course.'

By the river Styx in his brother's kingdom, by its banks where the pitch-black waters and whirlpools boil, he nodded to confirm what he'd said, and his nod caused all Olympus to tremble. No more was said. Jupiter rose from his golden throne, and the gods that dwell in the sky formed up on either side to lead him out to the door.

118–259   The Italians continue to attack the Trojan camp. That night Aeneas is sailing towards the Tiber with Tarchon and his thirty Etruscan ships filled with troops. He is met by sea-nymphs who warn him that his camp is under attack. The sun is beginning to rise.

260–314   Aeneas returns.

And now from where he was standing high in the stern he could see the camp of his fellow Trojans. At once he held out the shield on his arm, to blaze in the sunlight. The Trojans on the wall raised a great cheer: fresh hope restored their spirits, and they let fly a shower of spears. Turnus and the Italian commanders could not understand it, until they looked round and saw ships backing up to the shore, and the whole sea alive with boats gliding in.

Flames flared from Aeneas' helmet; a river of fire poured from its plumes on top, and great flashes streamed from the golden boss of his shield. It was just like seeing on a clear night the trail of a comet glowing blood-red and ominous, or the bright star Sirius rising, which brings with it drought and plague to unhappy mortals, and saddens the sky with its sinister light.

But brave Turnus' confidence was quite unshaken: he was sure of seizing the beaches before them and of stopping them landing. He spoke out to encourage, even rebuke, his men: 'At last the chance you have longed for is here, the chance to crush them in combat. Brave men have the winning of war in their own hands. Let each one of you remember his wife and home, and repeat the great deeds which won our fathers their fame. Let's face them right at the edge of the waves while they're scared and barely on shore, with their footsteps still shaky. Fortune fights for the brave.'

Meanwhile Aeneas was disembarking his men from their high-sided ships; many of them watched for the waves to break and subside before launching themselves into the surf, while others slid down the oars.

Tarchon had spotted a place on the shore where the water looked deep enough and the waves were not breaking and booming, but flowed up smoothly over the beach, and quickly steered straight for it, calling to his comrades: 'Come on, you're the men I chose! Throw all your weight on the oars, they won't break. Come on! Lift the boat out of the waves – plough up the enemy shore with the bows, let the keel cut its own furrow! I don't even care if we wreck the ship in getting ashore, so long as we're safely on land.'

At Tarchon's rallying cry the men rose to their oars, drove their ships through the foam up onto the Latin soil, till the bows came to rest on dry land and the ships were all beached unharmed – except one, Tarchon's. It struck on a shoal and hung on a treacherous reef, tilting this way and that, defying all the waves could do, till at last it broke and threw its crew into the water: they struggled ashore through fragments of oars and broken benches, as the backwash sucked at their feet.

Without wasting a moment Turnus fiercely rushed his troops down to the shore and stationed them facing the Trojans. The trumpets sang out. Aeneas led the attack against these rustic companies and, an omen of success, scythed down the Latins, slaughtering Theron, a massive warrior who was brave enough to attack him – Aeneas' sword went through his bronze chain-mail armour, on through the gold-broidered tunic, and opened a gaping wound in his side . . .

315–439 That was the start of the carnage. Virgil relates the gory details of Aeneas' successes. The whole passage which follows is marked by vivid descriptions of gruesome wounds as Virgil emphasises the horrors of war. Though Aeneas is himself unstoppable, elsewhere the fighting is more evenly matched. At one point Pallas' Arcadian cavalry is in difficulties, till Pallas leads them back into the fighting. Turnus hurries to meet this new danger.

440–504 So Turnus cut his way through the melée in his swift chariot, and catching sight of his men cried: 'You can stop fighting now! I'll deal with Pallas, alone – he's mine, mine alone!

If only his father were here to see it!' His companions obeyed his orders, and withdrew from the field.

Young Pallas was puzzled by the Italian withdrawal, and heard Turnus' arrogant words in amazement, but carefully sized up his opponent's gigantic physique, sternly eyeing each feature. Then he answered the cruel prince's challenge: '*I* will win praise today for stripping *you* of your armour, or else for my noble death – my father won't mind which it is! To hell with your threats!' As he moved on to the field, a chill ran through the hearts and blood of his fellow Arcadians.

Turnus jumped down from his chariot and strode out to fight on foot, like a lion that has seen from some look-out a bull in the plain below, pawing the ground for battle, and leaps down to kill it. The sight of Turnus advancing was equally frightening. When Pallas thought he was in range of his spear he made the first move, hoping that fortune would help him for daring to tackle a more powerful enemy, and sending a prayer to high heaven: 'Hercules, I beg you by the welcome my father gave you, by the table at which you sat, though a stranger, help me in this mighty enterprise. Let Turnus' dying eyes see me strip off his blood-stained armour, let his eyes close in death on my victory!'

Hercules heard the youngster, and stifled a great groan deep in his heart, then gave way to hopeless tears. Jupiter spoke to his son, with comforting words: 'Every man's day is fixed – every man's life is short and is over once it has gone. But to increase his fame by his deeds, that's what a brave man *can* do. Beneath the great walls of Troy died many a son of the gods, even my own son Sarpedon. Now Turnus is called by his fate, close to the end of the life that's allotted him.' So he spoke, and turned his eyes away from the land of the Rutuli.

But Pallas, with all his great strength, flung his spear, and snatched his bright sword from its scabbard. The flying spear burst through the edge of the shield and, piercing the breastplate high up where it covered the shoulder, just grazed Turnus' huge body. Then Turnus, carefully aiming his oak-shaft steel-tipped spear, hurled it at Pallas, and cried: 'Now see whose spear goes deeper!' And the quivering spear-point smashed through the middle of Pallas' shield, for all its layers of iron and bronze, or the layers of bull's hide that covered it, and piercing his protective breastplate gored into his mighty breast. Pallas tore out the weapon, warm from his wound – but in vain: his blood and his life poured out by the same path, together. He toppled over onto his wounded breast, with his armour clanging about him, and collapsed with his blood-flecked lips on the enemy soil as he died.

Then Turnus towering above him cried: 'Remember my words, Arcadians, and take them to Evander. I send him back Pallas, in the state he deserves. If there's honour in a tomb or comfort in burial, Evander can have it. But the welcome he gave Aeneas will prove very costly!' So he put his left foot on the back of the corpse, and tore off the great heavy sword-belt. . . he gloated at having it, delighted to have won such a prize of war. But the minds of men are blind to the working of fate and their future, nor do they know when to stop when luck's on their side. The time was coming when Turnus would give anything never to have laid a finger on Pallas, when he would hate this prize and the day he won it.

505–768   Aeneas loses all control and rages over the battlefield, ruthlessly slaughtering great numbers of the enemy to avenge Pallas' death. Ascanius breaks out of the encampment by the beach, and lifts the siege. Juno obtains permission from Jupiter to save Turnus from the fighting, but only for a short time. She makes a ghost of Aeneas which runs away from Turnus. He pursues it onto a ship and is trapped on board when Juno draws the boat out to sea. Turnus is whisked off to his home town, Ardea; on realising how he has been deceived he bitterly curses the gods for luring him to desert his comrades.

Mezentius then takes Turnus' place, leading the attack on the Trojans, and becomes as murderously successful as Aeneas in killing his enemies, 'striding over the battlefield like a tornado'.

769–832   Aeneas and Mezentius meet in single combat: Mezentius' son, Lausus, is killed when he intervenes to save his father.

Aeneas caught sight of him in the long line of his men, and went out to meet him. Undismayed, Mezentius stood steadfast and solid, awaiting his fearless enemy, judging with his eye the range of his spear: 'Now let my hand – that's all the god I need! – and this spear poised to strike, be with me now! I'll strip the armour from that robber's corpse and give it to Lausus to wear, as a trophy for defeating Aeneas.' With these words, he hurled the spear hissing on its way through the air, but it glanced off Aeneas' shield in its flight and struck noble Antores, standing nearby, between rib and thigh – he was a friend of Hercules who had come on a mission from Argos, joined Evander and settled in Italy. As the poor man lay stretched on the ground, from a wound meant for Aeneas, he gazed at the sky as he died, dreaming of Argos, the homeland he loved.

Then noble Aeneas threw his spear, which went through Mezentius' round shield with its curved triple sheets of bronze, the three linen-backed layers of hide, and came to rest low in his groin, though most of its force was spent.

Elated at the sight of Mezentius' blood Aeneas at once drew his sword from its sheath, and savagely leapt at his disconcerted enemy. On seeing him Lausus groaned in anguish for love of his father, and tears rolled down his cheeks.

I shall not let Lausus' heroic act go untold, nor the cruel ill luck of his death; he was a young man worthy of remembrance.

Mezentius was backing away, disabled and hampered by the enemy spear stuck in his shield as he dragged it away: out leapt Lausus to take his part in the fighting. As Aeneas gathered himself, raising his sword to strike, Lausus parried the blow with his own sword, holding Aeneas off, to buy time. His comrades rallied, yelling, behind him to let Mezentius withdraw from the battle, covered by the shield of his son, and tried to intimidate Aeneas by long-range shooting. Aeneas was furious, but stayed safely tucked under his shield. It was like being bombarded with hail in a storm, when ploughmen and labourers scamper out of the fields, and travellers crouch in some safe retreat, by the bank of some river or under the brow of a rock, as the rain pelts down and they wait for the sun to return, to get back to their work. So Aeneas withstood the hail of spears pouring down on him from every direction, waiting for the storm to blow itself out, all the while taunting Lausus and threatening him: 'Why throw your life away by fighting right out of your class? Playing the dutiful son has made you blind to the danger.'

But Lausus kept up his frenzied assault: now the furious rage of the Trojan commander boiled up still higher, and the Fates gathered in the last threads of Lausus' life. For Aeneas drove his powerful sword straight through the young man's body, buried it right up to the hilt. The sword-point went through his shield – too light a weapon for so fierce a spirit – through the tunic his mother had woven of soft gold thread, soaking its folds in blood.

The soul sadly flew through the air to the shades below, leaving the body behind.

But when Aeneas saw the expression on the dying man's face, now growing noticeably paler and paler, he groaned deeply in pity, and stretched out his hand to touch him, and the picture of his own love for his father came into his mind. 'I too know the call of duty; what honour can I give you, to match your honourable deeds and stirling character? That armour – you were proud of it – keep it. Your body I'll send to join your ancestors' ashes and shades; perhaps that means something to you. You will find some consolation, at least, in falling to great Aeneas' hand.' And Aeneas rebuked the slow-moving comrades of Lausus, and was himself the first to pick up the body, its neatly dressed hair fouled with blood.

833–908   Mezentius hears of his son's death, and prepares to face Aeneas. No matter how dreadful his life may have been, his death is heroic and dignified.

Lausus' father, meanwhile, was cleaning his wound with water from the river, and stanching the blood, leaning his back on a tree trunk to recover his strength. His bronze helmet hung from a branch nearby, and his ponderous armour lay quiet on the grass. The picked men of his guard stood round him as gasping and weak he was washing his head, with his beard flowing over his chest. He kept asking about his son, kept sending messengers for him, with orders that he should come back to his anxious father. But Lausus' friends were tearfully carrying his lifeless body back on his shield, the noble victim of a noble bout. Scenting disaster, Mezentius realised, even before they drew near, what their grief meant. He covered his grey hairs in dust, raised both hands to heaven, then clung to the body.

'Was I so fond of life, my son, that I let you take my place in the front line, you, my own son? Is your father to be saved by your wounds, kept alive by your death? Ah, now at last I know, to my sorrow, how bitter is exile, how cruel the blow! I was hated and banished from the home and throne of our ancestors, and stained my son's name with my crimes. Long before now I should have made amends for my countrymen's hatred; no form of death could be too harsh for my guilt. Yet I am still alive. I have still not left the light and the world of men, but leave them I will!'

So saying he raised himself on his injured leg; though the depth of the wound slowed him down, resolutely he told them to bring him his horse. This animal was his comfort and pride; it had carried him home victorious from all his wars. He spoke to the mourning beast: 'Rhaebus, our lives have been long, if "long" can be used of anything that's not immortal. Today you shall bring back Aeneas' head, and that famous armour drenched in his blood, as our prize; you will join in vengeance for Lausus' agony: or if that is beyond us, you will die when I die, brave friend, you'll never accept, I am sure, a new master, and never a Trojan.'

He spoke, climbed up and, as often before, settled himself on Rhaebus' back, in each hand clutching sharp javelins, with his bronze helmet gleaming and sporting its horse-hair plume. So into battle he charged, his heart a turmoil of shame and madness and grief. Three times he shouted out 'Aeneas' and Aeneas acknowledged the challenge and joyfully prayed: 'May Jupiter, Lord of the gods, and Apollo on high grant me my wish! Come on! Fight!' Without more ado he levelled his spear and went out to meet Mezentius.

And Mezentius cried: 'You murderer! Now that you've taken my son, do you think that you can terrify me? You found the one way to destroy me! I've no fear of death, no respect for the gods. Enough talking, I've come here to die, but first I have these gifts for you.' And at this he hurled a spear at his foe, then planted another, then another, in Aeneas' shield, wheeling around him in a slow, wide circle, but the gold shield-boss stopped them all.

Three times he galloped round Aeneas, keeping his shield-side towards him, shooting at him. Three times the Trojan warrior turned his bronze shield with its forest of spears to face him. Then, tired of these wearisome tactics, of pulling out so many spears, and worried at fighting on unequal terms, on foot, he carefully planned his movements and at last lunged forward, flung his spear, and struck Mezentius' charger at the side of its forehead. Up reared the stallion, its forefeet flailing the air, threw off its rider, then crashed down on top and pinned him, and lay with its head stretched out, shoulder broken.

Trojans and Italians together lit up the sky with their shouts. Aeneas ran forward, snatched out his sword, and stood over him: 'Where is that bold man Mezentius now, where is that savage ferocity?'

144

And Mezentius staring up at the sky, sucked in a breath and recovered his senses: 'Why do you mock me by threatening death? There's no sin in killing me: "kill or be killed" were the terms on which I came to fight, and Lausus made no agreement with you for anything different for me. I have one request, if beaten enemies are allowed to ask favours – let my body be buried. My people's implacable hatred surrounds me, I know; protect me from their fury; let me lie in the same grave as my son.'

He spoke, and deliberately offered his throat to the sword, and his life poured out over his armour in a wave of blood.

Book XI

At the beginning of the Book the Trojans are left in command of the battlefield. Aeneas sends Pallas' body back to Evander, and a twelve-day truce is concluded between the two sides to allow them to bury their dead.

The Latins hold a council of war. First, a report is heard from the embassy which had been sent to ask for the help of Diomede, announcing his refusal to risk meeting the Trojans again. Then Latinus recommends peace, on almost any terms. Drances supports him, and urges a duel between Turnus and Aeneas to decide the war. Finally Turnus argues that the war is neither already lost nor hopeless; however, he is ready to face Aeneas in single combat. But while they are talking, news comes of a Trojan advance, and the war is renewed.

The remainder of the book is largely devoted to a cavalry battle. The Italian forces are led by a warrior princess, Camilla. It ends with her death and the defeat of the Latins. Night overtakes both armies encamped in front of Latinus' city.

❦❦❦❦

The tide of war turns strongly in favour of Aeneas. He is now shown as a resourceful and confident commander, while fear and hopelessness spreads among his enemies.

Camilla is a heroic warrior in her own right, very like Turnus in her courageous and impetuous behaviour. Yet her bravery is all in vain, and her death is made all the more pointless as it is caused by the cowardly and cunning Arruns, who kills her without ever having the courage to meet her in battle face to face.

Characters

Aeneas
Diomede
Turnus
Camilla
Tarchon
Arruns

 1–99 After dedicating Mezentius' armour as a trophy to Mars, Aeneas arranges a guard of honour of 1,000 men to take Pallas' body home to his father Evander. A delegation comes from the Italians asking for a truce.

100–21 Envoys had just arrived from Latinus' capital carrying olive branches, with a request that Aeneas should let them have the bodies of the dead, lying all over the fields where they'd fallen, to give them a formal burial. There was nothing to fear, they explained, from men who were defeated and dead. Let him show mercy to them, for they had welcomed him warmly once, and had offered their daughters in marriage. Their request could hardly be refused, and Aeneas readily granted it. He added these words: 'What unkind twist of fate involved you in this great war, Latins, and made you reject my friendship? You have asked for peace for the dead, for the victims of war – I would prefer to give it to men still alive. I only came here when destiny told me to make my home in this land. I'm not making war on the people – it was your king who refused our friendship and preferred to rely on Turnus' army. It would have been fairer if Turnus, not they, had died. But if what he wants is to finish the war by force, to drive out us Trojans, then he should have met me in single combat, when the best man, or the one with the gods' support, would alone have been left alive. Go now, and take your poor friends to the funeral fires.' They stood there, impressed by his words, looking in each others' faces, but still with nothing to say.

122–280 The envoys thank Aeneas, and a twelve-day truce is arranged. Evander receives the funeral procession: bitterly lamenting his own inadequacy and his son's death, he finishes by asking Aeneas to take vengeance on Turnus. Both sides bury their dead. Resentment against Turnus and his betrothal to Lavinia, which has caused all the suffering, grows in Latinus' city. Then the embassy which had been sent, laden with gifts, to ask for Diomede's help against the Trojans, returns and reports failure. Diomede refuses to fight the Trojans again in any circumstances, and gives the Latins the following advice.

281–93 'Those gifts which you have brought from your home-land for me, give them to Aeneas. I've stood in front of those pitiless weapons of his, and fought face to face. I know from experience, believe me, how he towers above you, thrusting his shield, how he hurls his spear like a whirlwind. If two more heroes like him had grown up in Troy our luck would have been reversed, the Trojans would have sailed for Greece, and Greece would be mourning now. During all that long wait outside the tough Trojan walls it was the strength of Hector and Aeneas that prevented the Greeks from winning, for nine whole years. Those two were outstanding in courage and prowess at fighting, but the nobler man was Aeneas. Accept the best terms you can get – don't let it come to war.'

294–433   These words increase the Latins' despondency. Latinus declares that the situation is hopeless and proposes to make peace, either by giving up some of his land to the Trojans, or by building ships for them to sail elsewhere. These peace proposals are supported by Drances, an enemy of Turnus, who now makes a personal attack on him, and ends by calling on Turnus to accept Aeneas' challenge to single combat. Turnus angrily accuses Drances of cowardice, then suggests that there is no need for pessimism. Their situation, he says, is by no means desperate, but continues in the following words.

434–42   'Well, if the Trojans want me, and nobody else, for combat; if that's what you wish, and if I'm such an obstacle to our people's prosperity – I am not so unused to victory that I would refuse any venture that offered so great a reward. I have the courage to face him, even if he should out-fight the famous Achilles himself, and, like him, put on armour that Vulcan himself has made. I am Turnus, as brave as any of the heroes of old. I dedicate my life to you and to Latinus, whose daughter will be my wife. So Aeneas challenges me, not anyone else? I pray that is true!'

443–97   The debate in the Latin headquarters is interrupted by news of a Trojan attack. Turnus gives instructions for action, his promise to meet Aeneas single-handed swept away in the alarm, then leaves the debate.

498–519   Camilla offers help. Turnus gladly accepts it, and asks her to meet Tachon and his Etruscan cavalry while he himself lays an ambush for Aeneas and the Trojan infantry.

Camilla rode to meet him at the head of her Volscian troops: right by the gate the princess leapt from her horse, and following her lead, all her men swung down from theirs. 'Turnus,' she said, 'if bravery gives me the right to feel confident, then I'm confident enough to promise to take on the Trojan mounted brigade, to fight the Etruscan cavalry single-handed. Let me tackle the first danger of battle; you stay here with the infantry and guard the walls of the city.'

Turnus' eyes were fixed on the awesome girl: 'Princess, you're a credit to Italy! What can I say to thank you? What can I do to repay you? But now, since nothing can daunt your courage, share this task with me. There is a report – and the scouts we've sent out confirm it – that that criminal Aeneas has detached his light cavalry with orders to clear the plain, while he himself is coming, by a steep unguarded pass through the mountains, to sweep straight down on our city. I am planning an ambush where his route's overhung with trees, to block each end with armed troops. You must face the Etruscan cavalry and engage them. You'll have Messapus with you – he's a hard man – the Latin squadrons and Tiburtus' troops. Take over the command yourself, and part of my burden.'

520–647 While Turnus is setting the ambush, the goddess Diana tells one of her nymphs, Opis, that Camilla is fated to die, and that Opis must take vengeance on the man who kills her. Then the cavalry skirmish outside the walls develops into a major battle, with first one side, then the other, appearing to gain the upper hand.

648–720 Camilla in battle. Virgil describes the deaths of twelve men, though only four are recounted here.

648–58 Through the thick of the slaughter, like an Amazon with one breast bared for battle, her quiver slung over her back, Camilla went storming. She hurled volley after volley of quivering spears, or whirled in her hand, untiring, a great battleaxe, while the golden bow, the weapon of Diana, rattled on her shoulder. Even when driven to retreat she twisted the bow round and let loose a stream of arrows. Around her were picked companions, the maiden Larisa, Tulla, and Tarpeia wielding her bronze battleaxe, Italian girls whom the godlike Camilla herself had chosen to grace her side, to serve her faithfully in peace and war.

664–68 Who was the first, who last, to fall to ferocious Camilla? How many men did she strike to the ground to die?

Euneus, Clitius' son, was the first: as he turned to face her she pierced his unprotected chest with her long pinewood spear; he coughed up rivers of blood as he fell, bit the bloodstained ground and died, doubled up over the wound.

690–720   Then she killed Butes and Orsilochus, two of the best of the Trojans. Butes was hit by the point of her spear as he rode past her, where his neck showed between helmet and breast-plate, for his shield was low on his arm, off guard.

She outmanoeuvred Orsilochus by running away and riding in a wide circle, then wheeling in a tight curve inside so that the hunted became the hunter. Then she rose in her stirrups, smashed her strong axe with repeated blows through his armour and bones, though he begged her and prayed for mercy: his warm brains ran down his face from the wound.

Aunus' warrior son from an Apennine farm was the next: he stood rooted to the ground in terror at the sudden sight of her – a real slippery character while the Fates let him cheat and deceive. Now when he saw there was no chance left of running away from a fight, that he couldn't escape the princess's eager pursuit, he started to use his cunning and skilful tricks. 'What's so fine,' he said, 'in a female fighter, if she relies on the strength of a horse? Send away that chance of escape, meet me on equal terms on the ground, fight me on foot! You'll soon see whose puffed-up boasts will betray them!'

Stung by his words and fired with fierce indignation, Camilla handed over her horse to one of her comrades, and unafraid faced him on foot with the same arms as his – a drawn sword and a simple shield. But he thought his trick had succeeded, and instantly tugged the reins round and galloped away in flight, raking his speeding steed with iron spurs.

'You conceited fool, do you think that's clever? It's no use trying tricks like your crafty old father, you slimy creature! They won't save you and get you back home to him!' So saying, Camilla, running fast as fire on her nimble feet, caught up with her enemy's horse and seized its reins, brought him to bay and took full vengeance in his hateful blood.

732–40   Tarchon is inspired to fight with greater ferocity, and tries to arouse his troops.

'What are you scared of, Etruscans? Aren't you ever ashamed? Don't you ever *do* anything? What's turned you into such great cowards? It's a woman that's sending you flying and routing your ranks! What are your swords for? Why carry arms and not use them? You're quick enough to jump into bed and make love, or to join in the dance when the music calls! Well, wait for the feast, for the wine and fine food – if that's what your hearts are set on – for the priest to announce good omens, for the scent of fresh meat to invite you to join in the sacrifice!'

741–58   Tarchon dashes into battle, and captures one of the enemy.

758–67   Inspired by Tarchon's success, the Etruscans followed his lead and charged to the attack. Then Arruns, his fate already decided, clasping his spear, circled around Camilla and cunningly kept pace with her, despite her speed, looking for the most promising chance. Wherever the impetuous girl went in the heart of battle, there Arruns appeared, furtively tracking her. If, after some successful skirmish, she withdrew from the fray, he stealthily turned his swift horse towards her, constantly circling her, trying to get close, now here, now there, poising his unerring spear, relentless.

768–77   Camilla's attention is caught by a rider and horse both splendidly armoured.

778–806   Perhaps she wanted to hang up his golden arms in a temple, or to capture his gold apparel and, when she went hunting, wear it herself – Camilla picked on this one man in the turmoil of battle and, blind to all danger, followed him through the ranks, without thought for herself, fired with a womanly love for beautiful things won in war.

Arruns seized his chance at last; aiming his spear from where he was lurking he prayed to the gods above: 'Holiest of gods, Apollo, warden of sacred Soracte,[1] we Etruscans are foremost in paying you homage; keeping a pile of pine logs blazing to honour you, we worshippers, firm in our faith, walk through the flames, placing our feet on the burning embers. Apollo all-powerful, grant that I may wipe out this disgrace with my spear. I don't ask for spoils, for a trophy for defeating a woman. I don't want booty, my other deeds will win me fame; if I can but strike down this ruinous pestilence, I'll cheerfully go home unhonoured.'

Apollo heard, and decided to give him part of his prayer; the rest he threw to the fleeting winds. He granted his wish to catch Camilla off guard and kill her, but denied him a return to his home in the mountains – these were the words that the winds snatched away. So the spear shot from his hand and hissed through the air; the Volscians all intent kept their eyes and hearts on the princess. She was aware of no sound or wind from the spear as it sped towards her, till it struck beneath her naked breast and lodged there, driven deep and drinking her maiden blood. Her comrades ran to their mistress in alarm, and caught her as she collapsed.

806–15　Arruns, with fear and joy combined, gallops away to hide in the lines of soliders.

816–31　Camilla, dying, tugged at the spear, but the iron blade, deep in her side, was fixed in her ribs. Drained of blood she drooped lower as her eyes drooped down in the chill of death and the colour ebbed from her cheeks. With her dying breath she spoke to Acca who, faithful beyond all the rest, was the only one to share her thoughts: 'Dear Acca, I can do no more, this cruel wound is the end of me; everything's going dark all round me. Hurry, and take this last message to Turnus – he must take over the battle from me, and keep the Trojans away from the city. And now, goodbye!' As she spoke she let go the reins, and helplessly slid to the ground. Then slowly her body grew cold and let go of life; she lowered her neck and head, overcome by death, dropping her weapons, and her soul with a sigh of complaint fled to the shades below.

836–915　The nymph Opis shoots Arruns down, as Diana had instructed. The Italians are driven away in flight, and their city besieged. Turnus, on hearing of Camilla's death abandons the ambush, and returns to the city.

Note to Book XI

1　**Soracte**　A mountain about 20 miles (30 km) north of Rome, on which was a temple of Apollo. The custom of walking through fire is still quite common in the modern world.

152

Book XII

Turnus, provoked by the low morale of his troops, announces that he will keep his promise to fight Aeneas in single combat, and asks Latinus to arrange the conditions. Neither Latinus nor Amata can dissuade him. The two heroes prepare to fight, and the soldiers of both sides gather to watch. Juturna, Turnus' sister now appears. (She had been turned into a nymph, and given immortality, by Jupiter.) She persuades the Rutuli to attack the Trojans, despite the truce agreed, saying that this is the only way to save Turnus' life and their own future independence. Aeneas tries to stop his men from breaking the truce, but when he is himself wounded by a stray arrow the fighting resumes. When Venus heals the wound and Aeneas rejoins the battle, Juturna disguises herself as her brother's charioteer, and succeeds in preventing Aeneas from coming near him.

Aeneas and Turnus deal out death indiscriminately, till Aeneas is encouraged by his mother to assault the Latin capital. Queen Amata is horrified by this turn of events, and believing that her conduct is responsible for it commits suicide. At this Turnus, shrugging off Juturna's opposition, rushes back to the city and tells the Latins to leave him to decide the issue in single combat.

In the first phase of the struggle the sword which Turnus is using breaks, and Aeneas' spear becomes stuck fast in a tree-trunk. When Juturna brings Turnus his own sword Venus frees her son's spear from the tree, and the warriors turn to face each other again.

In Olympus Jupiter tells Juno to take no further part. She agrees, but begs him not to allow the Latin race to disappear. He agrees, and compels Juturna to leave the battlefield, desperately miserable that she cannot save her brother. The duel starts again, and Turnus is defeated.

❦❦❦❦❦

In this final book, significantly, all the action is left to the four main pairs of characters, Jupiter and Juno, Latinus and Amata, Turnus and Juturna, Venus and Aeneas.

 1–17   Turnus speaks to Latinus.

When Turnus saw that the Latins were cast down by defeat, saw all eyes upon him demanding he keep his promise, he was fired with an unbending resolve, and his spirits lifted. Just as an African lion, caught in the open, only moves to the attack when hunters have dealt him a grievous wound in the breast – then he delightedly tosses the great mane on his neck, fearlessly breaks off a spear which the huntsman has lodged in him, and roars defiance from bloodstained jaws – so did a violent passion kindle and glow in Turnus, and he snarled out his fury at Latinus.

'I'm not playing for time! There's no reason for those cowardly Trojans to break their word or withdraw their challenge; I'm on my way! Carry out the ritual, sir, and settle the terms. Either I'll send him to hell, that Trojan, that Asian runaway – the Latins need just sit still and watch, and unaided I'll prove with my sword that we are not cowards – or else he shall see us defeated, and marry Lavinia.'

18–53   Latinus tries to calm Turnus down and advises him to marry someone else; Lavinia ought to marry Aeneas, as both the oracle and popular opinion had originally demanded: he is prepared to make peace anyway, so there is now no need for Turnus to risk his life. But Turnus is completely unmoved. Then Amata tries, with no more success.

54–80   But the queen, appalled by the danger of this new turn in the fighting, in floods of tears clung to the hot-headed Turnus, just as ready to die herself: 'Turnus, by these tears, I beg you, by whatever respect for Amata you have in your heart – you are the only hope and comfort of my sad old age, Latinus' honour and throne are in your hands, our whole failing house depends on you – this one thing I beg: don't fight the Trojans! All the risks you face in that combat face me as well. If you die, I too will end this life I hate. I shall not be a captive, I'll never see Aeneas marry my daughter.'

Lavinia was listening to her mother; tears fell down her burning cheeks, as a deep blush flamed and spread all over her glowing face. It was like a piece of Indian ivory stained with blood-red dye, or white lilies catching the colour of scarlet roses in a bouquet, as the colours came and went in the young girl's face.

Turnus was overwhelmed with love as he looked at Lavinia. Now even more passionately determined to fight, he answered

154

Amata briefly: 'Dear mother, please, don't send me off to such a stern contest with tears, that's bad luck indeed! I am Turnus, I cannot back out because there's a risk of dying! Idmon, take a message to that Trojan tyrant – it's not one he'll like. As soon as the light of tomorrow's dawn blushes pink as it climbs the sky, let him hold back his Trojan forces; let both sides enjoy an armistice while we two settle the war with our blood, and decide in the field whom Lavinia shall marry.'

81–695   As Aeneas and Turnus are standing ready for the battle, fighting breaks out again amongst their troops, despite the oaths taken to guarantee peace. In the course of the battle Turnus hears that Amata has committed suicide. He calls his men back from the front, demanding the right to face Aeneas alone.

696–790   The scene is outside the walls of Latinus' city. Turnus has just told the Latins to stop fighting and leave everything to him.

So they all drew aside, and left a space clear in the middle.

But on hearing Turnus' name Prince Aeneas hurriedly left his attack on the walls and lofty citadel, brushed aside any cause for delay and broke off all operations. Jumping with joy at the thought of fighting Turnus, he drummed sword on shield, a terrible sound, looking as big as a mountain which proudly lifts its snow-capped peak to the sky when a wind storms through the shivering tree-tops. Now the Rutuli, Trojans and all the Italians turned their eyes on the pair, even the men guarding the battlements or battering the walls below with their rams, and put down their weapons. Even Latinus marvelled to see these two mighty warriors, born in different parts of the world and brought face to face here to fight it out with the sword. And they, as soon as a space was cleared on the plain, tried a spear-throw from a distance, then ran forward to attack till their shields met with a clang of bronze. The earth groaned in sympathy as they rained down blow after blow from their swords as chance or courage directed them.

Sometimes in a great forest, high up in the hills, two bulls charge head on into a vicious fight: the herdsmen back off in terror, the rest of the herd stands silent in fear, the young cows wondering which of the two will be king of the forest and lead the whole herd. The two bulls savage each other with powerful charges, heaving and thrusting their horns till their necks and shoulders are awash with blood, and the forest re-echoes their bellowing. In just the same way Aeneas and Turnus clash shield to shield, and the air is filled with the din. Jupiter himself holds the scale up, balanced and level. He puts the fates of the two separately into the pans, to see which would be doomed by the struggle, whose death would weigh the scale down.

At this moment Turnus, thinking he had a safe chance, lunged forward and rose to his full height as he lifted his sword, and struck with all of his strength. The Trojans and Latins cried out in excitement, and all eyes were riveted on them. But the treacherous blade snapped in mid-blow, and failed the furious Turnus – no hope of escape but to run. So swifter than wind he ran when he saw his right hand unprotected, saw that the sword was not even his! In his hurry, so goes the story, when mounting his chariot at the start of the battle, he snatched up the sword of his driver Metiscus, failing in his excitement to pick up his own sword, that had once belonged to his father. For a long time this blade had been good enough, when the Trojans were straggling away in defeat. But when it came up against the weapon that Vulcan had forged, then, being man-made, it shattered like brittle ice at this blow, and the pieces gleamed on the golden sand. Desperately Turnus tried to escape to a different part of the plain, running in circles erratically, this way and that, for the Trojans had formed a dense ring all round them, and the wide marsh cut off one escape-route and the high walls another.

Now Aeneas, though he was sometimes slowed down by the arrow-wound, when his legs gave way and denied him their usual speed, still chased eagerly after him, almost treading on the heels of his terrified enemy. It was like a deer-hunt, when a hound has the stag trapped in the bend of a river, or hemmed in by the nets with their scare of scarlet feathers, and chases it, running and barking. The stag then frightened by the scarlet snare and the height of the river bank, again and again scurries back over its tracks. But the spirited hound sticks to its trail, mouth agape, always about to seize it, seeming to seize it and snapping its jaws, but baffled and biting thin air.

Then what a roar arose! The river banks and pools re-echoed all round, and all heaven rang with the thunderous cheers. Yet Turnus, even as he ran past them, cursed all the Rutuli, calling each man by his name, and demanding his own well-tried sword.

But Aeneas threatened death and destruction for anyone who went near him, and threatening to wipe out their city terrified the trembling Rutuli, and even though he was wounded kept on after him. Five times round they ran, then back another five times, forward and backward, for the prize they were chasing was no small sporting trophy – it was Turnus' life-blood at stake.

Now there had once stood here, as it happened, a wild olive tree, with leaves that were bitter to taste, sacred to Faunus, the god of Laurentum. From ancient time it had been revered by sailors, for here, if saved from some shipwreck, they would hang up their offerings to him, and peg up the clothes they had promised him. But the Trojans had removed the sacred trunk of the tree without thought for all that it meant, so that Turnus and Aeneas might have a clear space for their contest. Aeneas' spear was stuck in the stump where the force of his throw had driven it, gripped fast in the tough clinging wood. Aeneas was now bent over it, straining to tug out the steel point with his hands, to catch with the spear the man he could not catch up on foot. Then, crazed with fear Turnus cried, 'Faunus, I beg you, have pity on me; and you, dear land of mine, hold fast to that spear, if ever I've paid you the respect which they have profaned with war.'

He spoke, and his call for the help of the god did not go unheard. For Aeneas, long though he stayed struggling over the clinging stump could not, for all his efforts, loosen the bite of the tree. While Aeneas was fiercely tugging and straining, Juturna, immortal daughter of Daunus, changing again into the shape of Metiscus the chariot driver, ran forward and handed her brother his own sword. Venus was furious that the bold nymph should be allowed to do it; she came up herself, and tore out the spear from deep in the stump. Aeneas and Turnus then, both elated, with arms and spirits restored, one with his trusty sword, the other tall and fierce with his spear, stood facing each other, panting and ready for battle.

791–817   In Olympus Jupiter forbids Juno to interfere any more. Juno is aware that she has carried her opposition far enough, and at last agrees.

818–42   'Now I give in: I am leaving the war, I detest it. One thing I beseech you – there's no law of Fate to forbid it – for Latium's sake, for the dignity of your Latin people. When they have made peace, and confirmed it with a happy, yes, happy marriage, when they are working out mutual laws and agreements, do not compel the Latins, who were born here, to change their ancient name and call themselves Trojans. Don't make them change their language or dress. Let it stay Latium; let Alban kings rule them in long succession; let a breed of Romans arise, finding their strength in the Italian stock. Troy is dead: let it die, let its name die with it.'

With a smile the creator of men and all things replied: 'You are truly the sister of Jupiter and daughter of Saturn, such a storm of temper is boiling up in your heart! But come, put aside this anger, it's pointless. I grant your wish; you have won, and I surrender quite willingly. The Italians may keep their native tongue and traditions, and keep their name as it is. The Trojans will make their contribution by mingling their blood, but will then fade away. I'll blend in, as well, the customs and rites of Trojan religion, but make them all Latins, speaking one language. And the race that will come from this mixture of Italian and Trojan blood will surpass all other men, and even the gods, in goodness; no other people on earth will treat you with more reverence.'

Juno nodded agreement, and changed her whole attitude happily, then left her cloud and departed from heaven.

843–86   Jupiter now sends a Fury from hell down to the battlefield; in the guise of a screech-owl it flutters terrifyingly in Turnus' face. Juturna recognises that it is a sign from Jupiter that Turnus must die. Broken-hearted, she leaves her brother to his fate.

887–952   The final scene brings the death of Turnus. Aeneas sees the killing as vengeance for Turnus' arrogant cruelty to Pallas. Right to the end we may be expecting Aeneas to show mercy, but he cannot. The reconciliation in heaven was easy; not so on earth. There were no easy endings for the Romans of Virgil's day; there are none for us now.

Aeneas moved up to face Turnus, shaking his huge tree-trunk of a spear, then in savage anger cried; 'So why more delay now?

Why draw back at this time? We must settle this contest between us, not by running away, but with cruel steel, face to face. Choose any shape you like, call on any advantage of courage or skill that is yours. Fly up to the stars on wings, if you like, or hide underground in the depths of the earth!'

Turnus shook his head in despair: 'It is not your hot words that terrify me, fierce though you are, but the gods, and Jupiter's enmity.' Without a word more he looked round and caught sight of a huge rock, a huge primeval rock that happened to be lying on the plain where it had been set up as a boundary stone to settle a dispute about fields. Even a dozen picked men of the sort that the earth now produces could hardly have carried it off on their shoulders. But Turnus, a hero still, snatched it up in his anxious hand, rose to his full height, and with a run hurled it at Aeneas. But he felt quite unlike himself as he moved forward and ran, as he rose up and threw this enormous rock. His legs faltered, and his blood, growing cold, turned to ice. And even the rock which he threw, as it flew through the empty air, fell short and failed to strike home.

As in a dream, when sleep in the darkness has drowsily weighed down our eyes, we seem to run away, anxiously, faster, but we can't, and even while trying we fall down weakly; our usual strength has deserted us, and our tongue won't work, and not a sound, not a word, comes out; so Turnus, whatever he bravely attempted to do, was foiled by the Fury. Then in his heart his feelings veered this way and that; he gazed at the city, at his own Rutuli, he stumbled in fear, trembled at death's approach, saw no way to escape, no means of getting at Aeneas – his chariot and his sister who drove it were nowhere in sight.

As he faltered, Aeneas brandished his deadly spear, and seeing a favourable opening flung it from some way off with all his strength. The roar that rocks make when hurled from siege-engines was quiet in comparison – it was louder than the crack of a thunderbolt. It flew like a dark tornado carrying dreadful destruction, broke through the rim of Turnus' sevenfold shield, then laid open the edge of his breastplate. Hissing, it drove through his thigh, knocking him down to the ground on bent knee with its force. The Rutuli leapt to their feet with a groan that bounced back from the hills all around them, while the wide woods re-echoed the sound from their depths.

So was Turnus brought low, and humbly raising his eyes he stretched out his hand in appeal: 'I have deserved this, I don't ask for mercy; make the most of your luck. Yet, if you can be touched by the thought of a father's sorrow, a father like your father Anchises, then pity my father Daunus. Give me, or, if you prefer, my dead body back to my people. You have won. The Italians have seen me beaten and raising my hand in defeat. Lavinia is yours to marry. Carry your hatred no further.'

Aeneas stood fierce in full armour, and watched him, his arm by his side. Turnus' words more and more were beginning to sway him and weaken his anger when, high on Turnus' shoulder, he noticed the unlucky sword-belt and recognised the gleaming studs of the baldric that young Pallas had worn before Turnus had wounded and killed him. Turnus was wearing it over his shoulder as a mark of his victory.

Aeneas fixed his eyes on this prize which brought back his savage grief at Pallas' death. Burning with fury, terrible in anger, he cried: 'Do you expect to escape me when you are wearing my friend's equipment? With this blow Pallas destroys you, Pallas takes vengeance on your murderous blood!' With this he buried his sword in his enemy's chest in a passion of anger. The body went limp and cold, and his soul, with a sigh of complaint, fled to the shades below.

Published by the Press Syndicate of the University of Cambridge
The Pitt Building, Trumpington Street, Cambridge CB2 1RP
32 East 57th Street, New York, NY 10022, USA
10 Stamford Road, Oakleigh, Melbourne 3166, Australia

© Cambridge University Press 1984

First published 1984

Photoset, printed and bound in Great Britain by Redwood Burn Limited, Trowbridge, Wiltshire

Library of Congress catalogue card number: 84-1930

British Library cataloguing in publication data
Virgil
[Aeneid. English, Selections]. Selections from the Aeneid – (Translations from Greek and Roman authors).
I. Title II. Tingay, Graham III. Selections from the Aeneid IV. Series
873'.01 PA6801.A7
ISBN 0 521 28806 1

Maps by Reg Piggott